Contents

About the Author

Dominic Wyse LTCL, LRAM, GRSM (Hons), PGTC, MPhil, PhD, MA (Cantab) is Professor of Early Childhood and Primary Education at the Institute of Education, University of London. Prior to that, he was a Senior Lecturer at the University of Cambridge and Fellow of Churchill College Cambridge following a Readership at Liverpool John Moores University. His main research interests include the teaching of English, language and literacy. He has published many research articles and books. His books for students include the bestselling *Teaching English, Language and Literacy* (3rd edition, with Russell Jones, Helen Bradford and Mary Anne Wolpert, and published by Routledge). His books for researchers include *Literacy Teaching and Education: The SAGE Library of Educational Thought and Practice* (SAGE) and *The Routledge International Handbook of English, Language and Literacy Teaching* (edited with Richard Andrews and James Hoffman, and published by Routledge). Dominic has appeared on television, on radio and in print media in relation to his expertise on language and literacy teaching.

Acknowledgements

I would very much like to thank Jude Bowen at SAGE whom I have now known for more than 10 years – she is an exceptional editor. My very grateful thanks to all the students whose work is featured in the book – they were an inspiration to me. I also wish to pay tribute to Eve Bearne's influential contribution to the literacy field and for her insightful comments on earlier editions of this book. My warm appreciation also goes to all the people at SAGE who have been involved with the different editions of this book.

The book is dedicated to Steven Ford QC for his contribution in the form of a 15-year argument with me about grammar (which I claim he lost!) and for the two puzzles in the grammar chapter. It is also dedicated with fondness to the memory of Charlie Ford, who was never short of a viola joke.

How to Use this Book

The aim of this book is to help you to improve your writing. It has been written particularly for people who are studying education: the topics and examples have been chosen with those students in mind. However, students from a wider range of social science and humanities subjects will also find much in the book that will help them.

This third edition has been substantially adapted (to build on the success of the earlier editions), as a response to an analysis of readers' reports. The third edition has new sections that include new, fully worked examples of students' work, including tutors' comments. More work from both undergraduates and master's students has been added. To give an example of one of the substantial adaptations, a key theme of the book is how to write critically, one of the hallmarks of the best academic writing. You will find support for reading and note-taking to enhance critical writing, and the student examples of critical writing include reflections on the kind of language you need to use.

The way to navigate the book has also been made much clearer, particularly through a new, better organised contexts section where you can identify the topics you need help with and go straight to them. The new contents also reflect some reorganisation of the chapters of the book. The new advice on referencing provides the most up-to-date guidance from the world's leading guides, and includes a new section on the use of notes and bibliographies to add to the extensive guidance on the American Psychological Association's sixth edition of their guide to the author/date system. This chapter has been moved to the more appropriate place after considerations of reading widely, recording, and planning writing. The chapters on grammar and punctuation have been streamlined and combined. And, finally, a further reading list has been added at the end of the book.

The book is still divided into two parts. Part I helps you to see that good writing is closely linked with reading and thinking. Reading and thinking precede good writing but they also continue during the writing process itself. The nuts and bolts of the writing process are the focus for Part II.

One way to use this book is to read it all, think about the ideas and then try some of them when you do your next piece of writing. Another way to use the book would be to check the contents pages or summaries at the beginning of each chapter to find a topic that is of particular interest to you, read the chapter, and then try the ideas. The numerous examples of students' writing will enable you to compare your work with theirs. These will help you to realise that writing is hard work for all writers but it is something that becomes much easier with practice and thought.

The chapters begin with an overview of the topic. Key principles are outlined which should be used to guide your writing. To complement the text of the overviews, 'top tips' are offered, which, if you adopt them, will lead to quick improvements. The book also includes 'key facts' throughout. These will help to focus your mind on the essence of the concepts that are being covered. The final part of each chapter includes 'dos and don'ts' which help you to avoid common pitfalls.

What if you don't understand a particular term? The glossary at the end of the book consolidates and adds to the key facts to help you with this. The words included in the glossary are denoted with the symbol ❻ on their first occurrence in the book. And don't forget the index – you might find that a quick search in the index could save you a lot of time when trying to find a particular piece of advice about writing.

Finally, bear in mind that writers and publishers have different ways of doing things. For instance, there is more than one way to reference and to use some punctuation marks. Whether or not you follow my advice on these aspects, it is important to apply your chosen style consistently.

By buying this book, you have already done something positive; you've said to yourself 'I want to improve my writing'. If you take on board the messages from the book and apply them to your own writing, you are likely to see your writing going from strength to strength, and so will your tutors!

Part I

Reading and Thinking

1

Reading Widely

The single most important thing that you can do to learn more and to improve the chances of success on your course is to read widely. In order to help you to do that, this chapter gives guidance on the qualities of the different kinds of texts that you will read and explains why some are likely to help more than others. The important concept of *peer review* Ⓖ is introduced in relation to internet texts, academic journals and books.

You may have heard stories about people with no previous experience suddenly writing a bestseller. One day they sit down and, without planning, write for about six weeks solid, until a book is complete. With very little effort, they become rich beyond their wildest dreams. Do not believe these stories! When you look into the background of any successful writer, there is a history of writing experience behind them. It may be that they kept a diary; or perhaps they wrote a travel journal for each holiday, or edited a school fanzine. Many writers begin with a lot of hard work getting one short story published in a magazine; some writers have experience as a journalist, a teacher, an academic or some other job that requires regular writing. Whatever their background, all professional writers succeed by very determined hard work, the ability to learn from their failures and the understanding that becoming a good writer takes time.

Thankfully, you do not have to become a professional writer in order to succeed on your course, however there are lessons that can be learned from these people. What all writers have in common is that they have practised the craft of writing. But just as important, they have read widely the kinds of texts that they intend to write. This shows us that if you want to write brilliant assignments, you need to read similar texts. Examples from previous years' students can be helpful but in particular you should read published books and papers by experts in your subject. This is the kind of writing that is the best model for your own.

As a student on a course, you read for four main reasons:

1 You read to learn more about your subject, sometimes called 'the *field'* **G**.
2 Texts contain the knowledge that you need as part of your course.
3 Texts give clues that can help you in your writing.
4 Wide reading results in greater success on your course.

The second and fourth points are related. Any formal course assessment is designed to assess the level of your understanding of a particular topic. The knowledge required for the highest levels of understanding is contained in published texts. Therefore, you have to read these texts and show that you have fully understood them to achieve the highest marks.

However, the point that I want to emphasise is the third point: you must learn to read like a writer. After you have read a text to understand more about your subject, read it again in a different way. Read it with questions like these in mind:

- Who is the writer's main audience?
- What issues has the writer chosen to cover?
- If I list the main issues, does it help me understand the piece better?
- How does the writer organise the text?
- How do they use *subheadings* **G**?
- What particular words and phrases do they use?
- How do they refer to other people's work?
- What makes the first *sentence* **G**/first paragraph effective?
- What kinds of texts are listed in the *reference list* **G**; which ones shall I read next?
- How do they start the text?
- How do they end the text?

★ TOP TIP

Your understanding will be stronger if you read texts first hand for yourself (the *primary source* **G**) rather than if you read another text (a *secondary source* **G**) describing the primary source.

The relevance of wide reading to essays and other academic assignments is perhaps more obvious than to assignments that focus on practical teaching and evaluation. You might question how wide reading improves these teaching evaluations. Your own views and reflections on your practical work are important, but you also need to challenge your opinions by comparing them with the opinions of others. Often, people who publish texts about education have taught for many years in a variety of settings so they are likely to have more experience to draw on than you. This means that they often understand the issues in greater depth. When you read and understand their work, you can benefit from their knowledge and will subsequently understand the subject in greater depth yourself.

Where to start your reading

A tutor's *reading list* is a very useful place to start. If the list is good, it will be up to date and will recommend texts that are at the appropriate level for you. However, students frequently find that key books on the reading list have already been borrowed from the library. If you find yourself in this situation, don't despair, as there are various ways round it. Although your tutor will recommend specific texts, the authors of these are likely to have published other texts that might be useful. You can do a *search* ⍟ under the author's name (see Chapter 2) to find other things that they have published. Perhaps even more important than this is to remember that journals cannot be taken out of the library so you will always be able to access them. More and more, these are available electronically so you can sometimes access them from your home. Another option, apart from books and papers, is the internet. But before you decide which kind of text to read, you need to understand about the qualities of different texts.

 KEY FACT

A *paper* ⍟ is an article published in an academic journal. Some papers are presented at academic conferences prior to publication.

The internet is a vast information resource which features the whole range of texts, including texts that are offensive, texts that are inaccurate, and other texts with a very high level of accurate and useful information. The main weakness of the internet is that it is much easier to publish a web page without having to go through a process which evaluates its quality.

The process which some publications go through to ensure accuracy and quality is called *peer review*. For example, if an article is submitted to a journal that is peer-reviewed the article will first be briefly assessed by the editor. Then, if generally suitable for the journal, it will be sent to two or more experts in the field who will read the article and write a report, indicating if they think it is good enough to be published. The editor or editors will then decide on the basis of the reports whether to publish. Ideally, this process should be 'blind': in other words, the referees should not know who has written the paper (some journals even require references to the authors' own work in the reference list to be disguised or removed).

KEY FACT

Peer review is a process which involves experts evaluating documents such as journal articles to ensure that they are accurate, original and significant, and therefore worthy of publication.

The information available on the internet can be particularly useful when you are in the early stages of thinking about a topic. But even at this stage it is important that you are selective about the sites that you use. You need to find sites that are authoritative and trustworthy. Here is a list of the kinds of sites you might come across and some ways that you need to think about them:

- A site published by a single author. This might be the site of someone who is an enthusiast about the topic, and it can be fascinating and full of useful information. The problem is that there is no way of knowing how good the information is.
- A government site. This kind of site is very helpful when gathering information about current initiatives. The information about the government's own initiatives is likely to be accurate. Government sites very rarely feature criticisms of the government's own policies so you need other sources in order to develop your critical thinking about them.
- An independent organisation site. This can be very useful to compare with information on government sites. It is important that you find out what the organisation's purposes are because this will affect the information that they offer and the way they interpret this.
- Sites which summarise topics and provide links to other sites. These can be very useful but the quality of information varies. *Wikipedia* is fascinating in this regard. Wikipedia does have a peer-review process (anyone in the world!) but you don't know the expertise of the people doing the reviewing.

- Newspapers and other media sites. These are particularly valuable if the topic of your writing is the media itself. Reportings of research by media sites can be inaccurate and misleading so they should be used to take you to original research reports rather than as a *citation* ⓖ.

The *Times Educational Supplement* (*TES*), which can be found online, is a good example of a potentially useful site. The *TES* is a weekly summary of current events in education. The online archives also allow you to search for previous news. Let's say that you have been asked to carry out an assignment with the topic of assessment. On 13 May 2005, Joseph Lee published an interesting article in the *TES* about the 'hysteria' caused by a government report which claimed that too many children were not learning to read. The *TES* article was helpful because it alerts people to the report from government. The article also made the important point that children who achieve level 3 are not 'failing', they are actually pretty good readers. But, although this has some useful information, it is not as rigorous as a good academic journal article (as you will see in the section below on journals).

★ TOP TIP

Make sure you know the right way to refer to media articles:

Inappropriate: "Eboda (2004) shows that institutional racism is present in teams of football commentators." While this may or may not be true, the citation (see Chapter 3) is to a journalist who wrote a newspaper article, not a researcher who has published evidence on the issue.

Appropriate: "The issue of racism has been highlighted in the press recently in an *Observer* newspaper article" (Eboda, 2004). This comments on the way the newspaper covered the issue rather than using the newspaper as an authoritative source to support a point.

Journals

Let's look at our topic of assessment from the perspective of a good research journal. Peter Tymms asked the question, 'Are standards rising in English primary schools?' and published the answer to this question in an article in the highly regarded *British Educational Research Journal*. He concluded that independent measures showed that the gains in statutory test results (often called SATs) between 1995 and 2000 were not nearly as strong as some people were claiming (including the government) and that after 2000 there was no further progress (Tymms, 2004). The reason that you can have a higher level of confidence that this information is trustworthy is that the whole article went through the peer-review process. Another indicator of the quality of this particular article is the way that the author draws upon a range of objective sources of evidence, such as the results from standardised tests of reading, writing and mathematics, as part of the argument.

But how do we know that the *British Educational Research Journal* is a good journal? In the past, we would only know this primarily by making a judgement about the quality of its articles over time. The people on the journal's editorial board, who are usually listed at the front or end of the journal, are also an important indicator of the quality. Another indicator is that journals that are international in character normally have a high level of writing. But how do you know if a journal is international? In recent years, another indicator of journal quality has become more prominent. There are now companies who monitor the number of times that people refer to different articles (these are called citations – see Chapter 3). Calculations are then made about the rank order of journals in terms of the number of citations that have been made to the articles in them: the rank order is published in reports. Here is a list of some of the journals in the UK that usually feature in the reports:

- Teaching and Teacher Education
- British Educational Research Journal
- British Journal of the Sociology of Education
- British Journal of Educational Technology
- Gender and Education
- Educational Research (UK)
- Journal of Curriculum Studies
- Oxford Review of Education
- Educational Studies
- British Journal of Educational Studies

As with all league tables, things are not quite as simple as the list implies. In fact, there are various complications that have to be considered.

The list above reflects journals based in the UK in order of the total number of citations. But there are other categories that can be used to sort the journals, such as *impact factor,* which is the average number of times articles from the journal published in the past two years have been cited in the year of the journal citation report. Another problem is that some subject journals, such as those for music, are not featured in the list. Journals about the teaching and learning of reading, writing, mathematics and science are included because so many people are researching those areas.

Even if a journal has a higher number of citations than another journal in the list, it may not be included if that field of study is judged by the company who publishes the reports to be well represented.

And the final issue is that there tend to be a lot of American journals. In part, this is because there are many excellent American journals but it is also because America has large numbers of researchers who are likely to know their own journals better than others.

Partly as a result of these and other issues, different kinds of lists have been developed, for example *Scopos* (http://www.info.sciverse.com/scopus/ access). These kinds of lists are one possible source to help you decide what the better journals are when trying to decide which reading to prioritise.

Reading and citing the most appropriate journal articles is useful at all stages of higher education but is particularly important at master's degree level and beyond. However, although the *British Educational Research Journal* is excellent, it is unlikely to be the place where you will start your reading because the articles are written at the level of professional research-ers and academics. Peer-reviewed journals differ in the level of writing and the nature of their peer-review procedures. For example, the journal *Education 3–13* is also peer-reviewed, but not in the same way that the *British Educational Research Journal* is. It also tends to cover more profes-sional topics and is written in a way that you will probably find easier to read in the early stages of your course.

Books

The better journals explain the way that they peer-review articles as part of their 'information for contributors', and this is how we know that they are peer-reviewed. For books, things are a little more complicated. Most education publishers require authors to prepare a proposal for a book (and often a sample chapter) which is then sent to referees. The proposal is sent, not the complete text of the book. This means that what the author writes in the book, if it is published, may not be peer-reviewed. Some pub-lishers do send complete texts to be peer-reviewed and the author then has to respond to any suggested changes. But it is very difficult for you to know which publishers are the most rigorous. In addition to academic peer-reviewers, publishers of books also use likely readers of the book as peer-reviewers, such as teachers. Professionals bring a different kind of review that in general will focus more on the relevance of the book to pro-fessional practice.

Books can be very useful because they give the author space to cover a wider range of topics in great depth. This means that a really good recently published book can give you a very good overview of *the field*. This can be a very useful starting point for your reading, although locating such a book is not always easy.

⚷ KEY FACT

A 'field' is an area of study.

If you find this kind of book, it should have an up-to-date reference list, and this means that you can choose some of the references to read first hand.

The word *handbook* ⒢ when used as part of the title for an academic book can be important. The word has a different meaning from the everyday idea of a handy book. A really good academic handbook is typically international in scope so it will have contributors from around the world who are experts in the field. It also attempts to be comprehensive in order to establish a clear picture of the field at a particular moment in time. These books are usually edited collections, meaning that an editor or editors will have invited contributors to send in a chapter. The editors will then offer comments about the chapter to encourage the contributor to improve it and to ensure it fits well with the aims of the book. The editors and the contributors will already have a track record in the field and will usually have published widely so you can have more confidence that this kind of book is academically rigorous.

★ TOP TIP

Work towards using high quality journal articles in addition to books to support the points in your assignments.

If you find that some articles and books seem to be very difficult to understand at first, don't worry. Part of the process of learning is the growing ability to cope with more and more demanding texts. When I started work on my master's degree, I was advised to read research methodology articles. At first, it was as if some of the articles were written in a completely different language because I could barely understand them. In a way, you could say that they *are* written in a different language. The highest levels of writing in a subject use short key phrases to summarise complex ideas. The writers assume that their audience has knowledge of the field and so will not need certain things explained. In other words, all subjects have *jargon* ⒢. When you see the word 'jargon', you probably think about it negatively as something that people use just to sound good. It is true that jargon can be used sloppily. But when used well, it saves writers having to explain particular concepts in full and at length.

The final distinction that I want you to understand is the difference between texts which give guidance about practice and those which are more theoretical and include research findings. The practical books will be useful if your assignment expects you to show that you can think clearly about your practice. The more theoretical books can be used as a citation (see Chapter 3) to support your academic arguments in an assignment. Some books are very good at mixing *theory* **G**, research and practice, although these are less common. Typically, you will find that in education assignments you need to use a mixture of theoretical and practical sources.

DOS AND DON'TS

✓ Do

- read texts yourself first hand rather than relying on secondary sources
- use the internet in the early stages of an assignment to help you get to grips with the main issues
- read recently published texts before you move to older texts

✗ Don't

- use newspaper articles to academically support the points that you are making in an assignment
- leave your reading until the last minute
- rely too heavily on one text

2

Searching for Reading Materials

The choice of the most appropriate texts is a very important part of writing a good assignment. In order to find these texts, you need to have effective strategies for *searching* Ⓖ. This chapter explains how you can use library computer catalogues and the *British Education Index* Ⓖ to make your searches more efficient. The chapter also explains how you can record your reading to support critical thinking, a key feature of the best writing at university.

In Chapter 1, I suggested that your tutor's recommendations are a good starting point for your reading when preparing for an assignment. However, you might well ask, which text do I read first? My advice is to start with one of the most recently published ones. If the author has done their job properly, the text will include a really good reference list with a range of work in the field which you can follow up on.

★ TOP TIP

The first text(s) that you read should be from the same year in which you are doing your work. Look for the year of publication of the article or book. Try and find a text published in the same year in which you are working. If you can't then try the year before, and so on.

Let's now think about other ways to search for texts. The most basic search involves going to the library and looking along the shelves. Although I am going to show that there are better ways to search than this, there is one advantage of looking at the books on a library shelf. If you browse the titles and check the contents occasionally, you do at least get a feel for the kinds of issues that are being covered by books in the field. The big limitation of this method is that there are likely to be many books which have been taken out of the library by other students.

Another basic search involves visiting your local bookshop to see which books are available on the shelves. Publishers' websites are an important part of this way of searching and sometimes offer free download materials. Internet bookshops such as Amazon allow you to search by simple categories of books, and this can also help in the early stages.

A more efficient search can be done by using the library computer catalogue. Library catalogues (like all search tools) work on *keyword* **G** searches of titles, authors and other bibliographic information.

★ TOP TIP

If you cannot find the exact text on your tutor's reading list, try a search for the author's name. This could help you find other texts that are relevant.

 KEY FACT

A keyword or keywords will describe the topic that you are working on.
Search engines **G** identify keywords in computer files that hold information about texts.

Most library catalogues work in similar ways so I have chosen the one at the University of Cambridge as an example because it is one that I have used.

KEY FACT

Cambridge Library is a Legal Deposit Library (previously called a copyright library). It keeps one copy of each edition of every book published in the UK and tries to conserve them forever. There are five Legal Deposit Libraries in the British Isles:

- Bodleian Library, Oxford
- Cambridge University Library
- National Library of Scotland
- Library of Trinity College Dublin
- National Library of Wales

The library catalogue at Cambridge has a basic search and a more advanced search, which is called a *Guided Search*. There are many different libraries which are connected at Cambridge. The search window shows a box for your keywords and some categories which you can choose:

> Keyword Anywhere – this will search for your keyword in any part of the library record for a text
> Author – this will search for the name of an author
> Title – this will search for the title of a text
> Journal Title – this helps you to search for journals that are in the library
> Subject Heading – here, libraries assign their own keywords reflecting the subject that texts cover
> Boolean Search – this enables you to combine keywords using 'and', 'or' or 'not'; for example, 'grammar' and 'teaching'
> Classmark – this is a code which indicates where you will find the text on the shelves
> Date – this is the publication date.

Let's choose a subject that you might be preparing for an assignment: the teaching of grammar in primary classrooms. A basic search for titles using the keyword 'grammar' reveals a range of texts (see Figure 2.1).

Next, you have to think about which of the entries might be most useful so that you can avoid wasting time on irrelevant items. Table 2.1 explains how I would think about this in relation to the search shown in Figure 2.1.

So, from the first ten items in the list, number five is the only one that I might check. However, if we use a better search strategy we might get some more relevant references. Here's what happened when I used the combination of 'grammar' and 'teaching' in the more advanced 'guided search' which allows you to combine keywords in more than one search box (Figure 2.2).

The first two entries appear to be about practice and so would be worth a look if this was the main focus of your assignment. But what about texts that report on research? The *Grammar Papers* was published by the Qualifications and Curriculum Authority (QCA), so normally you would expect this to be about government curriculum policy because that was the role of the QCA.

TABLE 2.1 Relevance of items in initial search for term 'grammar'

Item number	Thoughts on relevance of text
Items 1, 2 and 3	Publication date too old as a starting point for reading.
4	Full library record reveals that this is mainly about secondary education.
6, 8 and 9	History focus revealed by the information about library location, for example, 'Anglo-Saxon, Norse & Celtic Library'.
7	Gender as a topic may be too specific at this stage.
10	More about assessment than the teaching of grammar.

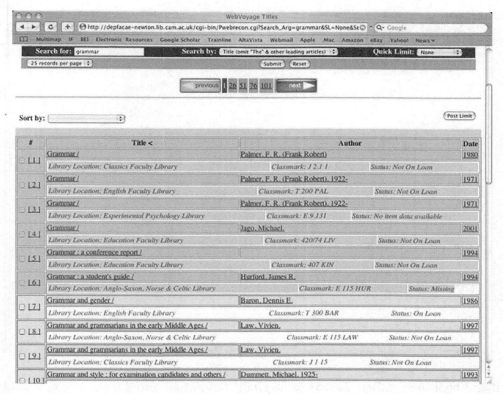

FIGURE 2.1   Cambridge University library catalogue basic search

However, the publication is a collection of papers which came out of a confer-ence that the QCA organised. One of these papers is a review of research into the teaching and learning of grammar (although, unusually, the author is not named). This is a useful text that I would definitely want to read for the assignment because not only does it cover research but it is also related to policy.

Overall, you can see that our brief search for books has given us two rea-sonable possibilities so far. In addition to reading them and recording some of the information (see later in this chapter), you should also check their ref-erence lists, and follow up on some of the useful ones to find further reading materials.

The main thing that the library catalogue search cannot locate is chapters about the teaching of grammar in edited books. For example, you often find that academic handbooks on the subject of the teaching of English may include a chapter on grammar, but library catalogues do not include the con-tents of books in their records. The only way that you can find these from a library catalogue is to make an assumption based on the title. For example,

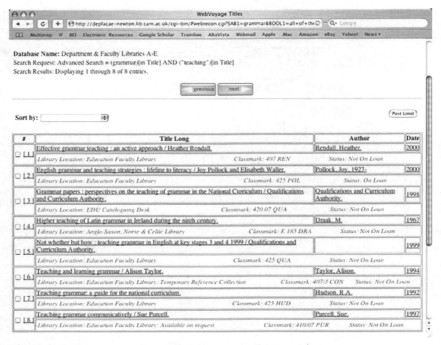

FIGURE 2.2   Cambridge University library catalogue guided search

if the book was called *Teaching English, Language and Literacy*, you would expect there to be a chapter on grammar. The other way to find chapters in edited books is if they are included in the reference list of another text.

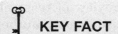 **KEY FACT**

Although a book called a 'handbook' sounds like it should be a relatively easy read, this is not necessarily the case. An academic handbook is intended to represent some of the best scholarship internationally in the field.

Although library catalogue searches are a good strategy in the early stages of preparation for an assignment, there are other more sophisticated ways that, once you are familiar with them, could save you time. It is also the case that as you progress towards the final stages of your course, there is an expectation that your reading will be carried out in more depth, and this will require better search strategies.

The British Education Index

One of the most useful tools for education students is the British Education Index (BEI) online. This enables you to find the titles of carefully selected peer-reviewed journal articles and theses (and some non-peer-reviewed work) in education from 1976 onwards. Most university education libraries subscribe to this service. You can normally access it on campus, or at home using an institutional password.

Indices like the BEI all work in a similar way by requiring keyword searches. You will probably be familiar with keyword searches on the internet by search engines like *Google Scholar* or *AltaVista* and, if so, will be aware how difficult it can sometimes be to find the particular piece of information that you want. This can also be the case with the BEI so the first thing to understand is that the particular keywords that you choose are vital in locating articles that are genuinely part of your topic and avoiding those that are not sufficiently related to your topic.

KEY FACT

Google has a separate search engine called Google Scholar. This can be more useful than basic Google in the early stages of preparing for an assignment.

Search for an author's name

Before I show you how to do a keyword search, let's start with a simple 'Author Name' search. Your tutor has recommended a book but all the copies are out on loan from the library. So you decide to check other things that the author has written, particularly journal articles, because you know that, provided your library subscribes to the journal, you will get hold of these electronically or be able to photocopy them. If you select the advanced search hyperlink next to the BEI title, the first thing that you see is Figure 2.3.

The advanced search offers three text entry lines, and to the right of each line is another text entry box that includes the option to restrict the keyword search to an author's name.

FIGURE 2.3   British Education Index advanced search window

★ TOP TIP

Here are the steps for a simple Author Name search:

1   Access the BEI through the website of your university or college library.
2   Select 'British Education Index' (as opposed to the Australian Education Index (AEI) or ERIC, the American version) by clicking the advanced search button.
3   Select 'author – AU' in the drop-down list of the right text entry box of the first search row.
4   Type in the surname (select correct name from auto suggest list).
5   Press enter.
6   Decide if any of the entries are relevant to your work by clicking on the title of the entry and viewing immediately or by ticking the boxes and viewing more than one entry.
7   Complete tick boxes to select any entries that are relevant to your work.
8   Save or email the results.

FIGURE 2.4   British Education Index search for author name Dominic Wyse

Let's stick to our example of the teaching and learning of grammar. If I key in my own name, part of the displayed list of articles includes the section in Figure 2.4.

One of the items in the list was an article called 'Grammar. for writing [*sic*])? A critical review of empirical evidence' which is clearly about grammar and is published in an educational journal, so it looked relevant.

🔑 KEY FACT

Sic ⓖ literally means 'thus'; in other words, although the word might look incorrect or questionable, it is quoted exactly as it was in the original version. (Unfortunately, the BEI hasn't quite got this right because the original is 'Grammar. For Writing?' – notice the full stop after grammar and the capital F.)

As I was the author of the article, I can tell you that it is about the teaching and learning of grammar and is a review of research with critical reflections on government policy, including the resource for primary teachers called *Grammar for Writing*.

A keyword search

Now, let's go back to a more sophisticated keyword search. If you are going to find some of the most relevant article titles, you need to choose the most appropriate keywords. To help with this, you can use the *Thesaurus* function. Let's continue with our example: the teaching of grammar. If you click the Thesaurus link and then type in the word 'grammar', you will see a list of *subject terms*. If you click on the plus sign for 'grammar' in the list, you are shown narrower terms, broader terms and related terms. You can use these to check if your keyword is the most appropriate.

The term 'grammar' had 1001 results. This means there are 1001 records that include the BEI special search term, 'grammar'. Unfortunately, that is too many records to read through efficiently so we need to limit the search. When I tried to limit the search to 'primary education (5–9/11)', it returned 0 hits for some reason but when I limited using the age group of children 0–12, it returned 154 hits which is almost a manageable number to read. Limiting again to 'scholarly journal' only reduced the number to 150. Finally, limiting to the date of 'last 3 years' reduced the list to a manageable number of 34 hits. However, when I looked down the list it was clear that the topics were more to do with linguistics than teaching grammar in primary classrooms.

One very useful strategy to limit your search is to combine the steps in the search history by using words such as 'and', 'or' or 'not'. Each one of the items in the search history is given a 'set'. You can combine items in the search history by simply entering numbers from the list separated by a word (such as 'and'), and then click the search button: for example 'S1 and S4'. By doing this to link the terms 'grammar' and 'writing skills', the number of items was reduced to 25.

> **★ TOP TIP**
>
> Limit your search by specifying particular years such as 'the last three years'.

Twenty-five records is certainly a manageable list to look through. The next thing to do is to check which of the items are most relevant to your work. One way to do this is to simply read the title of the article. The other way is to read the title of the journal. Quite a lot of the journals to do with grammar are about the teaching of foreign languages (such as *The International Journal of Language and Communication Disorders*) and so are not relevant to our current search. For our grammar teaching example, we primarily want education journals (although a journal on psychology like *The British Journal of Educational Psychology* will sometimes be relevant). Journals like *The British Education Research Journal* or *The British Journal of Education Studies* which have education in the title are the ones to check first. *English in Education* is an example of a subject-specific journal which often focuses on implications for policy and practice.

After we locate some items in the list that appear to be about the teaching of grammar, the full record of any item can be viewed and then saved in the

FIGURE 2.5   Example of indexing details for a journal article

same way that I described for the author search above. Figure 2.5 is an example of a full record for a journal article.

Having done your keyword search and established a list of relevant articles, your next job is to find out which ones are held by your library. By keying in the name of the journal into the library catalogue, you will find this out. Usually there will be a *hyperlink* to the website which provides access to the journal. If your library does not subscribe to the journal then you will have to complete an *inter-library loan* form. For a moderate charge, you will then be able to have the article sent to you by the British Library though this can take as long as two weeks.

KEY FACT

Inter-library loan is a service which allows you to borrow books or receive photocopies of journal articles that are not available in your library. There is usually a small charge for each item.

The BEI is the most appropriate index for education students but there are many other search tools that work in similar ways. For example, the *Social Science Citation Index* includes keyword search possibilities as does *Scopus*. There are also specialist collections such as the University of London, Institute of Education *Digital Education Resource Archive (DERA)* that contains all documents produced electronically by the government. Specialist education resources continue to improve so you need to talk to your university librarians about what currently are the most useful.

★ TOP TIP

Aim to limit your search until you can display 75 or fewer records.

KEY FACT

You will not be able to access a journal electronically if your library does not subscribe to the journal.

Reading and note-taking

Searching for reading materials is the first step, but the really important thing is what you do with the texts once you have found them. Put them in the trash? I'm only half joking here. You will need to skim read the texts that you find to check that they really are relevant to the questions you are pursuing as part of your work. Be ruthless about those that are not really relevant, return the books to the library and put the electronic articles in your computer trash.

Once you have found some texts that are relevant to your writing, you need to read them and record the useful information. The most effective way of doing this is to create an *annotated bibliography* : this is a list of the texts and notes about each text. If you prefer, this could simply be recorded by hand in a notebook but most people now use word-processed documents (for a free word processor, go to http://www.openoffice.org/) or spreadsheets.

The annotations are your notes about the texts. You should paraphrase (put into your own words), the ideas which you think are important. You could also copy exactly one or two direct quotes that you might use (make sure you record the page numbers because you will need them if you are to use the quotes in your work), but in general avoid too many direct quotes. The other important kind of notes you should make are your reactions to the ideas expressed in the text, including your critical and evaluative thoughts about the ideas expressed by the author in the text. For example, does the author provide appropriate evidence and/or logical argument to support their views? If they are reporting research, are the methods of research suitable to support (or *warrant*) the claims being made? Does the author crudely state political opinions or make assertions?

🔑 KEY FACT

An assertion is a personal opinion that is not backed up by appropriate evidence.

For each text that you read and make notes on, you should note the full reference information of author's name, year of publication, title, place and publisher, in the correct format (see Chapter 3). There are three reasons for this:

1   If the text is a book, you may want to re-read it at some point after you have returned it to the library. You will be able to find it again more easily if you have recorded the reference information.

2   If the reference information is correctly formatted, you will be able to efficiently incorporate it into the reference list of your completed assignment.

3   Accurate citation and references are one way to avoid plagiarism (see Chapter 5).

The most efficient way to record reference information is to use software packages that support this. In other words, you feed in the information and the software puts it into the correct format for you (see Chapter 5).

Critical reading and systematic recording

A simple annotated bibliography is a useful way to make notes on the texts that you read. However, in order to introduce a greater level of understanding, and to contribute to critical writing (see Chapter 10), you can introduce more sophisticated methods of systematic recording. In the world of professional research, techniques such as *systematic review* and *meta analysis* (a procedure for comparing quantitative outcomes from different research studies addressing the same topic) have been developed. You are unlikely to have the time or capacity to use these techniques, but the idea that you can be more systematic about the way that you record information from different studies is a valuable one. One part of this is developing your awareness of the qualities of different kinds of publications (see Chapter 1). But the main thing to do is to start to categorise your readings into groups of related studies that reflect the ways that you are thinking about your field.

Spreadsheets are well known for their functions in relation to mathematics but I have also found them very useful for systematically recording literature reviews, sometimes becoming an analytic tool. Spreadsheets have two main advantages over word-processed tables: (1) You do not need to add rows or columns because they are already there in almost limitless capacity; (2) You can easily sort the information in the spreadsheet according to the information in any one of the columns, for example alphabetically or numerically.

Table 2.2 illustrates one way that I have systematically recorded information from research studies. The question driving my interest was to what extent there is one most effective way to teach early reading. To do this, I acquired the research papers of 42 high-quality studies. I then categorised information from each of the studies so that I could compare their importance in relation to my overall question. Table 2.2 is a very much shorter version than the final spreadsheet which consisted of 25 columns, some with numeric information and some with textual information. Some

TABLE 2.2 Example of systematic recording of research studies

Author(s)	Age of children	Participants	Length of training	Nature of experimental comparisons	Reflections
Berninger, V. et al. (2003). Comparison of three approaches to supplementary reading instruction. *Language, Speech, and Hearing Services in Schools, 34,* 101–116.	7.0 to 8.7 2nd grade	'poorest readers' nominated by teachers. Each participating child was at least 1 SD below the mean on either word reading or pseudo word reading, and many were below that on the reading skill on which they qualified.	24 weeks, twice weekly x 20 mins	(a) explicit and reflective word recognition; (b) explicit and reflective reading comprehension; (c) combined explicit word recognition and explicit reading comprehension; or (d) treated control that only practised reading skills without any instruction.	Treatment delivered to pairs of children by 'tutors'. Clearly argues that comprehension instruction was beneficial – this included 'cueing at different levels of language' (p. 112). Differences between RD and normal readers – 'The results of this study of at-risk second-grade readers may not generalise to the initial stages of learning to read in a population of at-risk beginning readers ... Further research is needed on the developmental trajectory of at-risk students in learning to read. Children whose word reading skills are grade appropriate or advanced, or whose problems are specific to comprehension, may have responded very differently to the kinds of instruction provided. The results also generalise only to the specific kinds of explicit word recognition and reading comprehension training used' (p. 113).

of the thematic categories that emerged, and which influenced my writing, included: teaching as contextualised or isolated; length of training in weeks/less than one year/more than one year; participants as typical readers/struggling readers or readers with reading difficulties, etc. The critical aspect of the work came partly from the aim, which was to critically investigate if the government's claim that synthetic phonics was the best approach to early reading was backed up by research evidence. The other way that criticality emerged was through my reflections about each of the studies and their strengths and weaknesses in relation to my overall question and line of argument.

Table 2.3 shows a different approach to using spreadsheets as a tool for critical reflection. The example is an extract from a discourse analysis of about ten key curriculum policy texts. The research was about seeking to understand the way creativity was included and used in the texts. The stem 'creat' was used initially for a content analysis. By using the 'find' function, instances of any word that included the stem were located. These were then subject to an analysis of the semantic context for the use of the word, and a *critical analysis* ⊜ of the potential issues that arose as a result of the particular uses of the word in the policy texts.

How not to read

I have recommended that you should read the text and develop your own formats for synthesising information and recording your critical reflections. Unfortunately, there are a minority of students who adopt a rather damaging approach to texts. At the University of Cambridge library, they held an exhibition called *Marginalia and Other Crimes*. This showed the extraordinary ways in which some books are treated. Here is a list of the main kinds of damage:

- water
- fire
- ink
- coffee
- dogs
- mice
- children's stickers
- children's scribbling
- pigeon droppings
- pencil marks rubbed out (this always damages paper, however carefully carried out)
- pencil/crayon
- highlighter pens

TABLE 2.3 Example of discourse analysis of the New Labour National Curriculum of 2010 that was scrapped by the Conservative Liberal Democrat coalition government as soon as they came to power

Page number	Word/Phrase	Nature of section	Semantic context	Reflections
NA (online for all)	successful learners who are creative	The aims of the curriculum	Able to identify and solve problems	Only use of creativity in the overall national curriculum aims. Located in 'successful learners' column and preceded by 'essential' learning skills of literacy etc. Not creativity for intrinsic value?
	respond creatively	Essentials for learning and life: literacy	Able to respond creatively and critically to a wide range of information and ideas	Passive, i.e. responding to information? Comes after the more active using and applying literacy skills
	create information	Essentials for learning and life: ICT capability	Able to create information using technology to capture and organise data, in order to investigate patterns and trends ... create multimedia products	Lack of clarity in sentence but important because about creating things

- adhesive notes like Post-its (which lift the print and/or tear the paper)
- marginal authors who leave a signature and even an address (frequently not genuine)
- obscene comments and sometimes a response, rather like graffiti
- a series of numbers next to sentences underlined in pen to help with the points of an essay
- and worst of all … ripping out pages or cutting out photographs, which is regarded as theft. One business studies student said they thought that if they ripped out key articles in the top journal, they would have a competitive edge over their peers!

If you would like to see some photos of the damage, go to www.lib.cam.ac.uk/marginalia/. All of these are careless and thoughtless acts which spoil subsequent readers' experiences of the texts.

When you are reading and recording your thoughts about books, it is not necessary to read the whole book. If the book is an edited collection with a series of chapters by different authors then some of the chapters will be relevant to you and others will not. Other books written completely by one or more authors also do not need to be read from start to finish. You will need to use the contents and in particular the index to help you locate particular topics of interest. Skimming and scanning will also help you to skip content that is not relevant to you. However, you may find that in the early stages of your course it helps to read longer sections in full so that you gradually acquaint yourself with the particular language of your field.

Speed-reading

Some people argue that it is possible to learn to *speed-read* **G**; if this is true then it could be a helpful technique when preparing for assignments. Tony Buzan has written a popular book on the subject (Buzan, 2003). One of the techniques to help you to remember subject matter that he describes is the 'mind map'. This is like a spider diagram where you map the key concepts, issues and ideas. This visual representation is helpful to some people more than others. Essentially, like many such strategies, it is a summarising technique which leaves you with prompts that remind you about the issues. I was quite pleased to summarise all the key messages from his book in my simpler *text-map*:

Conditions for speed-reading:

1 Make sure that the time of day is good for concentration.
2 Set goals for times and the amount of material to be read.
3 Activate prior knowledge of the subject; remind yourself about what you know already and review easy texts on the subject.
4 Preview material first: skim and scan through the entire text.

5　Read larger chunks of text than you normally would, for example three lines at a time. 'Cyclopean' and peripheral vision can be used (a claim that you can use more of your eyes' capacity than you normally do).

6　Use one of the special eye movement techniques: forwards and backwards; zigzags; Ss; loops; a wave motion running centrally down the page; margin lines.

7　Check your comprehension when you reach the end of the section you have decided to speed-read. Make some notes.

Increasing speed:

1　Use a metronome to set the speed for lines read.
2　Time your progress on a chart.
3　Check your normal reading after each exercise.
4　Aim to increase your speed by 100 wpm each read.
5　Start with 2000 words in one minute, then increase the time to 4000 words in two minutes, and so on.
6　Speed-read whole chapters.

I have tried the speed-reading techniques and have found that they work to a certain extent, particularly if I am under pressure to read a set amount. I have not particularly tried to increase my speed other than the time when I first read the book and wanted to try the techniques. One of the problems that speed-reading poses for the academic reader is that a good assignment requires close analysis of the particular words and phrases of different texts in order to appreciate the nuances of language that are part of the arguments.

DOS AND DON'TS

✓ Do

- use search tools to be more efficient when finding texts
- learn to use the British Education Index
- record information using an annotated bibliography

✗ Don't

- rely entirely on searching the library shelves
- start your reading with older texts
- damage library texts by marking them

3

Planning for Writing

One of the main differences between speech and writing is the way in which writing can be planned. Careful planning is a powerful way to improve writing. In recognition that some writers prefer to plan in detail before writing while others just want to write first, this chapter recommends to you the idea of retrospective planning in addition to the merits of pre-planning.

All writers plan their writing. The planning may be mainly done in the head, or it may be written down in great detail, or more often it will be a mixture of the two. When I talk about planning, I mean planning that is done before you write the first draft. However, I am also going to talk about *retrospective planning* Ⓖ. This is planning that is sharpened up after you have written the first draft. It reflects the fact that writing and planning are closely related and to a certain extent happen simultaneously.

Writers' own accounts of their planning processes show that there are considerable differences in the way this is approached. Carter (1999) collected together the thoughts of a number of fiction writers and included reflections on the routines that they used for writing. Helen Cresswell, a prolific and talented author for both children and adults, describes her way of composing:

> With most of my books I simply write a title and a sentence, and I set off and the road leads to where it finishes. All my books are like journeys or explorations. Behind my desk I used to have this saying by Leo Rosten pinned up on the wall that went 'When you don't know where a road leads, it sure as hell will take you there.' When I first read that, I thought, that's

exactly it! That's what happens when I start on my books – I really don't know what's going to happen; it's quite dangerous, in a way. I often put off starting because it seems a bit scary. Yet at the end of the day, I feel that a story has gone where it's meant to have gone. (Carter, 1999, p. 118)

There are other writers who carry out written plans in detail before they write a word.

It is important that you develop a style of planning that works best for you. This style is likely to be refined as you develop your writing. My view is that the more experienced you become as a writer of a particular kind of text, or genre, the less written planning you need.

KEY FACT

To many people, the term 'genre' means a particular kind of fiction writing like 'romance' or 'thriller'. In education, the term refers to all different types of texts such as a newspaper article or poem or speech, and so on.

How planning changes as you become a more experienced writer

In the early stages of your development as a writer, you need to plan by writing things down more. But as you become more experienced, you can hold the equivalent of plans in your mind. Let me give an example from my own development as a writer. As part of the process of getting the contract for this book, I had to write a synopsis of the content. Here is the summary I wrote for this chapter:

Planning

The merits of planning writing will be discussed. Suggestions will be given on possible formats for planning including keyword paragraph plans. The concept of retrospective planning will be explained and examples given. Examples of professional writers' ways of planning will be discussed.

There is not much detail here. But the reason I am able to write approximately 3000 words from such a basic plan is to do with my experience and knowledge as a writer. I have written many books so I have a good idea about how to write non-fiction. I know the style and the structural possibilities. I am also drawing upon my extensive work with students. This knowledge helps me to think about the kind of text that I hope will be useful. My planning has not always been as minimal as this.

My first book proposal began its life as a plan represented by many sheets of A4 paper Sellotaped together and stuck on to a wall. Each sheet represented ideas about a particular section of the book. In a way, it was like a very detailed contents page with notes. The main thing I learned by doing this was to summarise a complete text relatively briefly, if a whole wall can be counted as brief! This is the main job of a writing plan: to summarise your whole text. It also provides a sequence of prompts to enable you to keep your writing moving forward. Although my first book proposal was not published, I learned a great deal from the process. My second proposal skipped the planning sheets on the wall stage and started with fairly detailed plans for each chapter typed into the word processor, which were used for the synopsis in the proposal. This time the idea was liked by three publishers. At the time, I was also getting to grips with the writing of research journal articles. For each section of the articles, I wrote keywords and phrases to help me decide what to include.

Overall, my written planning is now less than it used to be. However, one of the things that I still do, as I'm writing and as ideas occur to me, is add notes at the end of the text to remind me to cover particular topics and ideas. Sometimes I will use the word processor's very useful *comment* function to remind me to add something or check something later. Figure 3.1 shows a comment set out as a speech bubble in *page layout view*. Figure 3.2 shows the comment set out in *normal view* with the *reviewing pane* at the bottom of the window.

Some people recommend the use of visual techniques to aid planning. One of the most popular versions of this is the mind map or topic web. I think these are most useful in the early stages of your thinking when you are still trying to decide which areas to include in your assignment and which areas to leave out. However, you need to go a step further than this.

★ TOP TIP

Some people advise that the basic plan for an assignment is like this:
- Explain the points that you are going to cover.
- Make your points.
- Remind the reader about the points that you have made.

In my view, if you do this you will write a dull assignment because it will be repetitious. Here's a better basic structure:
- Introduce your topic in a way that will engage your main readers.
- Make your points.
- Conclude with the most important point you have made and explain the implications.

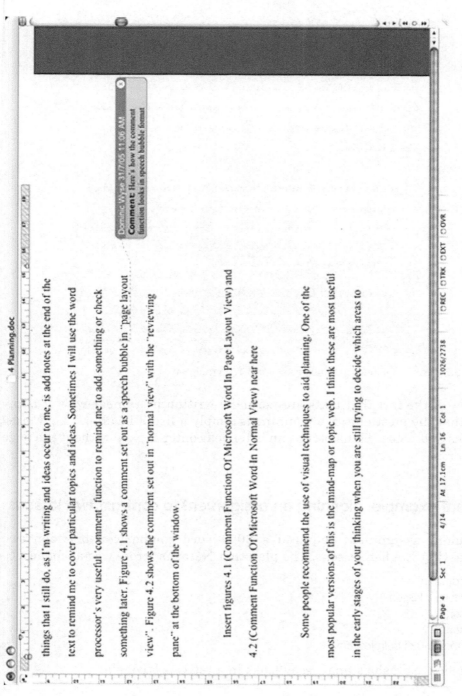

FIGURE 3.1　Comment function of Microsoft Word in page layout view

FIGURE 3.2   Comment function of Microsoft Word in normal view

In view of the fact that texts are normally written in a linear way, it is my view that the most effective planning is simply a list of headings, keywords/ phrases and notes. Think of it as an extended contents page without the page numbers.

Student example: planning an assignment to contrast two lessons

A student assignment required a 2000-word comparison between two contrasting English lessons. The plan that Natasha wrote was as follows:

Introduction
My literacy lessons
Lesson 1
Lesson 2
Comparison of both lessons

Here's how Natasha's final essay looks in a retrospective plan:

A comparison between a structured literacy hour lesson and a non-literacy hour lesson [title]

Introduction

Paragraph 1 (P1): Key features of the National Literacy Strategy (NLS) Framework for Teaching
P2: The segments of the literacy hour

My Literacy Lessons [subheading level 1]

P3: One sentence about weeks in the term that the two lessons were delivered
P4: The social characteristics of class
P5: The focus of the unit of work and the place of lesson 1 within this

Lesson 1 [subheading level 2]

P6: A description of lesson 1 with a focus on the literacy hour structure
P7: A brief comment about the restricting effect of the literacy hour structure, including reference to Collins and Marshall (2002)
P8: The behaviour of pupils; the level of support; differentiation, including for children with special educational needs (SEN); use of a commercial scheme

Lesson 2 [subheading level 2]

P9: A description of lesson 2 with a focus on open structure
P10: The flexibility of this lesson compared to lesson 1
P11: The response by pupils, particularly girls and pupils of different 'ability'
P12: The impact of mixed-ability groups
P13: Two sentences about the lack of need for adult intervention
P14: Pupil behaviour; pupil evaluations; reference to Collins and Marshall

Comparison of both lessons [subheading level 2]

P15: The teacher's role being 'directive' in the first lesson compared to the more pupil-led second lesson
P16: The quality of discussion between pupils and staff in the two lessons
P17: The second lesson being a 'joy to teach' compared to the first lesson; reference to Smith and Whitely (2000) regarding the prescriptive nature of the literacy hour; class teacher's comments about the literacy hour

(Continued)

(Continued)

> P18: Pupils' response and the difficulties of differentiating in the first lesson; one sentence on teaching styles; reference to Kempe (1999) on drama; mention of visual, auditory and kinaesthetic learning (VAK); references to problems for SEN children caused by the literacy hour and references to Beard (2003)
> P19: A two-sentence summary
> P20: Concluding critical points about the literacy hour
> P21: Concluding points about the need for more flexibility and creativity

KEY FACT

A retrospective plan is one that is written after you have done a draft of writing. It is a way of updating early planning to check that the structure of subheadings and paragraphs are in the appropriate sequence and that you are happy with the topics that you have selected.

The final essay had many good features – for example, the clear differences that were shown between the two lessons, the critique of the literacy hour and the important points made about speaking and listening. It could have been improved further by better planning (both pre-planning and retrospective planning) and redrafting. The subheadings are an important part of a plan because they divide the assignment into major sections. It is important to get the hierarchy of these correct and if you use the word processor's auto-headings, this can be a helpful aid to your planning. Natasha's *subheading* ❻ 'Comparison of both lessons' should have been a level 1 heading (at the same level as the 'My literacy lessons' heading).

Most of the paragraphs work well but you should always be suspicious about any paragraph that is only one or two sentences long; these nearly always reveal a point that is not fully developed. This was the case for Natasha's third and thirteenth paragraphs. Paragraphs 8, 14, 17 and 18 similarly failed to make their main points count, but this time because too many ideas were covered in the paragraph. As far as the overall structure was concerned, it would have been better to restrict the citations (see Chapter 5) to the early paragraphs. Reflections about classroom practice could then have been covered separately.

Natasha's overall approach to the assignment was logical. In order to compare lessons, it is necessary to think about them separately first, and then a comparison can be made. However, a higher level of thinking could have been shown if she had seen what she thought was her final draft as analysis, not as finished writing. Then, the next draft of writing could have built on her writing about the separate lessons by using themes, with examples chosen from both lessons, leading to stronger points. This is what is called 'synthesis' because ideas are integrated (or synthesised) through themes.

★ **TOP TIP**

Although analysis is a separate mental process, writing can be seen as a way to analyse. Look at your early drafts and ask yourself if they seem to be more analysis than final draft. If they represent analysis, you must rework in order to move towards clear findings and conclusions. The use of themes linked to subheadings can help to ensure that you have moved beyond analysis and description towards a synthesis of significant points.

A different way of planning the assignment

Let's consider a different way in which Natasha might have planned her assignment:

- Introductory material: key issues about the teaching of English and the literacy strategy covered in peer-reviewed articles and significant books. (After writing the complete draft, check to ensure that there is a link between these issues and those that emerge from analysis of the two lessons.)
- Introductory material: a brief description of context for two lessons including general differences.
- Theme 1: teaching style – nature of interaction and pupil discussion.
- Theme 2: pupils' response and learning.
- Conclusions: reflections on the merits of the literacy hour structure compared to other ways of teaching English. (Revisit at least one of the key citations from the introduction. Reflect on future classroom practice.)

If Natasha had planned like this, the assignment would have been clearly focused on reporting two main themes: different teaching styles in the two lessons and the different pupil responses. In a relatively short assignment of 2000 words like this one, it is important not to address too many issues. This risks not covering your points in sufficient depth.

If Natasha had improved her pre-planning and, in particular, her retrospective planning, it would probably have meant some reorganisation of her assignment rather than a great deal of new writing. Once re-planned, her new draft would have covered the issues as follows:

A comparison between a literacy hour lesson and a non-literacy hour lesson [title]

[Introductory material]

Paragraph 1 (P1) to P3: Key features of the NLS Framework for Teaching, including reference to books and papers to put this information in context
P4: The segments of the literacy hour
P5 to P6: Research and theory on teaching style
P7: Research and theory about pupils' response to the literacy hour (this may have to be omitted if over the word count)
P8: A general description of lessons including the way they fitted with the unit of work
P9: The characteristics of the pupils

[Theme 1:]
Teaching Style [subheading level 1]

P10: How Natasha's role as a teacher was different
P11: Opportunities for flexibility
P12: The nature of other adults' interaction
P13: The quality of discussion

[Theme 2:]
Pupils' Response and Learning [subheading level 1]

P14: Pupils' evaluations of the lessons
P15: The significance of drama supporting differentiation
P16: Particular difficulties for SEN children in the literacy hour

[Conclusions: Reflections on the merits of the literacy hour structure compared to other ways of teaching English]

P17 and P18: Critical points about the literacy hour
P19 and P20: Flexibility and creativity

I have put forward my view about the exact number and sequence of paragraphs in order to show the detailed planning that you may need to do. However, it may be that Natasha would decide on a greater number of paragraphs for some of the listed topics and fewer paragraphs for others.

You can see that proper planning of assignments leads to a better structure for the text. The structure of texts is important because it relates to your understanding of the topic that you are writing about. If you have a good structure, you will not only write a better assignment, you are also likely to retain the knowledge better because a good structure supports your memory by systematically organising the knowledge.

DOS AND DON'TS

✓ Do

- decide how you want to plan your assignments
- use retrospective planning to check the structure and logic of the writing
- remember that what you think of as a final draft may represent analysis rather than a finished product

✗ Don't

- be afraid to deviate from your initial planning
- think that you can submit an assignment with no planning at all and expect a high mark
- forget that the title and subheadings are an important part of the structure

4

Small-Scale Research Projects

Education courses often require you to carry out a piece of research and write it up for the final assessment. The writing up is a challenge which is much harder if the research has not been appropriately planned. This chapter shows you how to plan a piece of small-scale research. It concludes with an extensive example of how one student responded to tutor feedback on his research plans.

Most education courses include a significant piece of work for the final assignment. Frequently this requires you to carry out a piece of small-scale research and write it up. It is very common for the research to involve you doing some work in a classroom and reflecting on this. In Chapter 6, I offer a structure to help you write a report of your research for an assignment (sometimes called a *dissertation* ⓖ if it is a particularly important final piece). But before you can write a good report, you need to understand how to plan for and carry out a good piece of research.

It is helpful to define what we mean by research. Here is the definition used during the Research Assessment Exercise which universities and other research departments take part in:

> ... original investigation undertaken in order to gain knowledge and understanding. It includes work of direct relevance to the needs of commerce, industry, **and** to the public and voluntary sectors; scholarship, the invention and generation of ideas, images, performances, artefacts including design, where these lead to new or substantially improved insights; and the use of existing knowledge in experimental development to produce new or substantially improved materials, devices, products and

processes, including design and construction. It excludes routine testing and **routine** analysis of materials, components and processes **such as** for the maintenance of national standards, as distinct from the development of new analytical techniques. It also excludes the development of teaching materials that do not embody research. (Higher Education Funding Council for England et al., 2005, p. 8; original emphases)

You may have found that a bit mind-boggling because it is defining research in all fields. However, the most important sentence for our purposes is that research is "original investigation undertaken in order to gain knowledge and understanding". Research is also planned, systematic enquiry. You plan the research that you are going to do, you carry out your plans systematically and then you communicate or disseminate what you found out. Many courses require students to prepare a research plan and submit it to a tutor prior to carrying out the research. This may or may not be assessed, but whether it is or not, a plan can be an important tool in helping you do a good piece of research.

Before you plan your research, it is important that you read widely (see Chapters 1 and 2). At first, this reading will help you become aware of the issues in the field. It is also necessary in order to collect relevant references for your assignment. If you read research accounts, these can also give you ideas for the kinds of methods that you want to use. The best research deliberately extends previous work in the field in order to create new understandings.

What kind of research are you doing?

At master's degree level, it is not just the topic of the research that you will need to read about. You will also read about *paradigms* and methodology. In simple terms, a paradigm is a model or system for an area of knowledge. A particular paradigm will reflect the way that researchers who are committed to it think about and carry out their research. For example, qualitative research is regarded by some as a paradigm. Qualitative research often involves the analysis of interviews, observations and texts taken from natural settings. Qualitative researchers tend to think differently about research than, say, a researcher who favours experiments. You will come across other overarching terminology in the early stages. Here are two key terms: *epistemology* refers to how human beings know what they know – it is a theory of knowledge; *ontology* refers to theories of what makes up reality or of what exists. Your epistemological and ontological views will affect the way you think about research, including which methodology you think is appropriate.

The search for appropriate definitions for your methodology and the topic of your research is a necessary early stage of the research process. It is important that you understand and can define exactly what you are researching before your research starts. Because of the ever-increasing technical terms, there are now very useful research dictionaries and encyclopaedias to help you – for example, *The SAGE Dictionary of Social Research Methods*, edited by Victor Jupp, or the comprehensive *SAGE Encyclopedia of Social Science Research Methods*, edited by Michael Lewis-Beck, Alan Bryman and Tim Liao.

The rationale for your research

A good research plan will start with a rationale or reason for the research based on previous work. After the rationale, the next section of a research plan is usually the research questions. Research is stimulated by questions and/or a perception that something needs to be explored. Projects also often include a set of aims and/or objectives.

★ **TOP TIP**

Restrict your research plan to one aim and three objectives. This will help you to focus clearly and avoid planning research that will be unmanageable.

In the following example, you will notice the way that the aim and objectives are very closely linked.

Research Question: How does the UN Convention on the Rights of the Child impact on children in schools?

    Aim: To explore the nature and extent of children's participation in their school.

    Objectives:

- Analyse eight Year 5 and eight Year 6 children's views about participation in their school.
- Compare Year 5 and Year 6 pupils' views about participation with those of school council members.
- Reflect on observations of lessons and teachers' views in order to critically reflect on the views of pupils.

It is not always necessary to have both research questions and aims. Sometimes an introductory section which puts forward a rationale for the research, based on a reading of the literature, is sufficient to replace the research questions, provided there are clear aims and objectives.

In addition to the aims, objectives and questions, there are several other basic considerations that will require thought. The sample is a very important consideration for all research. In relation to the kind of research that you are likely to be doing, sample normally refers to the participants in the research, such as pupils or teachers, but for larger studies the sample might refer to schools or other settings in addition to the people involved. It is technically possible to have only one participant, something which has been done in ethnographic approaches. For instance, parents' accounts of the development of their child's reading and writing are a good example of this kind of work. Other research can require thousands of participants if it is statistical survey work. In addition to basic numbers in the sample, you will also need to think about the balance in terms of gender, race and socio-economic considerations. The important thing to remember is that the sample depends on the kind of research you are doing and, like all aspects of the methodology, serves to help you meet your research objectives.

Another useful thing to include in early planning is a timetable. The detail of a timetable forces you to think about a range of decisions that will need to be made. For example, if you are going to do some interviews, when and where will they take place? What do you need to do to get access to the site? How long will you spend at the site? Are you allowing enough time for ongoing analysis between your visits? Although timetables may well change once you start the research, it is helpful to give yourself an overview of how you will complete the work. The end of the timetable will include time for writing up the research and a final completion date.

You will also need to think about the kinds of data collection tools and methods that you are going to use. Once again, it is important to consider your objectives because the methods chosen should be the ones that are best suited to helping you to achieve them. There are many good introductory texts on research methods and, as space precludes a full account in this book, I have chosen to give an example of some of the issues to do with ethics because these are particularly important to consider when working with children.

★ TOP TIP

Look at the guidance for writing a dissertation in Chapter 6. The methods section shows a series of aspects that you should include. Most of these will need to be covered briefly in a research plan.

Ethics

One of the important dimensions of research with children is ethics. Professionally funded research with children requires that research proposals be submitted to an ethics committee. This is a committee of people who have expertise in ethical matters and who will decide if the research is appropriate to be carried out with children. Some universities even require undergraduate research proposals to be vetted by an ethics committee. There is a complex set of issues to be considered when you are thinking about the ethics of your research (this book can only provide a summary of some key issues; see Alderson and Morrow [2011] for a comprehensive account in *The Ethics of Research with Children and Young People*).

Children have rights of their own, which are complemented by general human rights legislation. The UN Convention on the Rights of the Child ensures that children have a right to participate in all matters that affect them. This means that if you are doing research with children, they must give their own consent. In order to give their consent, they must understand as much as possible about the research, as appropriate to their stage of development.

For example, you can say things like: 'The research I would like to do is about ... You do not have to take part if you don't want to and you will not be in trouble if you decide not to take part ... You can stop doing the research at any time ... The only people who will know your real name as part of the research will be the researcher and the researcher's teacher (their tutor) ...'.

Schools can be a particularly difficult place for children to exercise consent. Too often, teachers, who, under the law, are *in loco parentis* (which means they can take decisions as if they were a parent), oblige children to help with research without really asking for their consent. This can put you as the researcher in a tricky position because it is your duty to make sure that you have informed consent from the children. Gaining consent is particularly challenging with young children because of their general level of understanding, but even nursery children can understand a straightforward explanation about the research that you are doing and can be asked if they would like to take part. You can also explain to them that they are not going to be in trouble if they don't want to be involved and that they can withdraw at any time during the research. Parental consent is also necessary for research with children.

Confidentiality is another important ethical issue. All names should be fictionalised in any written reports. You should be honest and clear with the children about who is going to know their views. As a student, you and your supervisor will know about the children's views. Technically it might be possible to anonymise your data to the extent that even your supervisor does not know the names of the participants but this is probably not necessary, provided it is made clear to the participants. For undergraduate research, it is usually better if all data are destroyed once the research is complete. At the very least, data should be kept safely and securely so that any promises about confidentiality are not breached.

Research carried out by professional researchers that looks at 'controversial' topics like abuse or discrimination, or that involves children with special needs, always requires particularly careful thought. People who have carried out studies about abuse have recognised that the conversations that are held during interviews can lead to further trauma because of the memories that are stirred up. Researchers in these situations need to be trained in counselling or should have organised professional support for those participants who might need it. It is also possible that children might disclose information about being abused, a situation that would require the researcher to contact the local social services department. In this case, confidentiality cannot be maintained and written agreements with older children make this clear. Child abuse is not a suitable topic for inexperienced researchers and you should take advice from tutors if thinking about other kinds of research in controversial areas.

Strong arguments have been presented which suggest that research that is ethically appropriate should result in demonstrable benefits to children. One way of achieving this is by involving the children themselves in the research. The highest level of involvement comes when children carry out the research themselves, from planning to finished product. However, the supervision of such work requires a high level of skill, knowledge of the research process and knowledge of how children might work within such a process. Lower levels of involvement are possible. Kirby (1999, p. 46) suggests that for the different stages in the research process, six levels of involvement by children can be considered:

- none
- being informed
- expressing a view
- influencing a decision
- being a partner in a decision
- being the main decision-maker.

When you are planning your research, you should have reasons for your decisions about the level of involvement of the children.

Alderson (1995, p. 2) presents a useful list of ethical topics – accompanied by sets of key questions – that need consideration when carrying out research with children:

1 the purpose of the research
2 costs and hoped-for benefits
3 privacy and confidentiality

4   selection, inclusion and exclusion of participants
5   funding
6   review and revision of the research aims and methods
7   information for children, parents and other carers
8   consent
9   dissemination
10 impact on children.

The best research takes account of all the items on this list (with the exception of number five for research which is not funded). There are always potential benefits and potential costs for participants in research. Apart from health and safety considerations, costs can include time, inconvenience, embarrassment, invasion of privacy, sense of failure, or coercion. Benefits can include satisfaction, increased confidence or knowledge, and time to talk to an attentive listener. When you undertake research, ensure that it is well planned, systematically carried out and ethically appropriate. If this is done, there are benefits for participants and researchers.

Student example: thinking about a research project

It is rarely possible for tutors to closely annotate students' research plans because this is very time-consuming and they have to deal with many students. This is something that I have tried in the past, but I found that arranging a meeting with students and discussing hard copies of their draft proposals face to face was more efficient. To conclude this chapter, I offer the following example of a student's research plan which I *was* able to annotate. The students were given a simple list of headings that, as a minimum, they should cover in their research plan:

- research question(s), aim and objectives
- sample/participants
- access
- timetable
- data collection methods
- ethical considerations.

When you do the final writing up for a piece of research, there are many more sections that you need (see Chapter 6). A research plan is much more basic: you need to show the methods that you are going to use in order to work out that the research is feasible. At this stage, you are not usually required to write a lengthy rationale which includes references, but this will be required in the form of a literature review in the dissertation.

In the boxes below, you can see how one student, David, approached the task of the research plan. The comments in bold are my response to the first draft of his plan. (Although the comments are mainly criticisms, there are many positive features about this draft which I communicated to the student in the message of my email.)

David's first draft

First draft

Research question(s)

- Does the target group agree with recent literature and media suggesting that there is more pressure on young people nowadays to achieve academically well in exams?
- What effects do SATs have upon the children and their teachers? i.e. child's self esteem and opinion of schooling, the teaching methods demonstrated in the class-room (teaching towards passing a specific exam rather than teaching children what they need to know about a particular subject). Increased pressure upon teachers to gain good results from their pupils – what effect does this have?
- How does the education system differ as a whole, nowadays to before the introduction of SAT's **(no apostrophe)**, and what impact does this have upon the concept of childhood? i.e. children have less time to experience the freedom of being a child, lack of play, pressure and focus on academic achievement – possible effects?
- Is the early introduction of education into a child's life an advantage – discuss different education systems with good and bad points, for example, some European countries don't start children at school until the age of 7. **(These questions are too broad)**

Aim

To identify and discuss the opinions of 12-year-old children who have experienced the implications of early exams in their education, and compare these findings to the recent literature and media texts (see below) regarding this issue.

Research objectives

- To gather and analyse the views of 12-year-old children who have completed SAT's and the views of their teachers, head teacher, and if possible an examiner.

(Continued)

(Continued)

- To compare these views to what the literature and media texts suggest about early exams in a child's education **(this is not really an objective because it is a normal part of all research)**.
- To examine the impact of these exams upon the children, their teachers and possibly their parents, the education system, and the concept of 'childhood' as a whole. **(Limit this to children and teachers?)**

Methodology

Sample/participants

I wish to carry out my research project with 20 pupils, if possible 10 boys and 10 girls. I would also like to include two teachers – one male and one female, the head teacher and an examiner **(how will you get access to a test examiner?)**. Depending on the results of these findings, I may also speak to some of the parents **(No uncertainty, please. I would suggest leaving the parents or balancing the numbers of participants from each group)** and discuss whether they feel under more pressure to tutor their children at home from an early age due to the ever-changing education system.

Access

I have good communication links with my old high school so if my research topic is approved I should be able to use this school, and the pupils and teachers to help me throughout the duration of my research study **(but the tests are done in primary school. Perhaps you are planning to study the tests for 14-year-olds?)**.

Timetable

Yet to be completed. **(I need to see this)**

Data collection methods

I wish to carry out individual informal interviews with a few children – four or five – in my target group to gather their own opinions about SAT's, and possibly include a brainstorming discussion with the whole group about the effects that their exams had on them **(I like this combination of individual and group interviews)**. This will be useful as they can bounce their ideas off each other, and I will gain a more in-depth insight into their true thoughts. I would also like to give each child a questionnaire to complete using facial scale assessment **(necessary for 12-year-olds?)** and open-ended questions. I think these will be useful as the pupils may find it easier to express their comments and ideas about a certain aspect of the SAT's process, rather than if I was to talk to them face to face.

(Continued)

(Continued)

When researching the opinions of the adults involved in this study, I wish to interview them separately to gain a different perspective on SAT's and their possible effects on children and teachers.

Ethical considerations

Before completing the collection of this data, I will ensure that each participant is fully aware that the information given to me will be kept strictly confidential, and my study will not be used as a public document. They must also have signed a *consent or assent form* 🄖 to show that they understand the aims of my research, and know that they have permission to leave the study process at any time. My target group has been chosen so as not to discriminate against any individual, with an equal number of boys and girls, and male and female teachers.

The first draft usefully raised some issues to think about. One of the most important of these concerned the scale of the research. You will find that you get excited by issues that you want to research. But often these early ideas are too broad for the kind of small-scale research that you are able to do. You need to really focus on a small, manageable area. Students sometimes think that this might be boring but, on the contrary, research which is tight and well focused is more interesting because the tutor and the student learn from a more rigorous exploration. Part of my advice in relation to manageability was to suggest a smaller sample. Although David thought about this, in the end he decided to stick with his idea of interviewing parents in addition to the other participants.

Another of my comments was about the style of writing. Although a research proposal requires you to speculate about how you are going to carry out your research, you have to make a firm decision about what you are going to do. Some students include language such as 'I may decide to …'. It is better if the writing reads like a definite plan, even knowing that the tutor may suggest further changes.

David's second draft

For the second draft, I was conscious of the approaching deadline for the proposals so I decided to use the reviewing function of the word processor which includes *Track Changes* 🄖. In the example below, the boxes/bubbles in the right margin show the text which I suggest for deletion. Text that is underlined is my suggested replacement.

2nd Draft

Title of Research: The impact of statutory tests upon young people, parents and teachers, and the concept of childhood.

Research Question (s)
(a) Does the target group agree with recent literature suggesting that there is more pressure on young people nowadays to achieve academically in exams?

Aim
Assess the impact of statutory testing on 12-year-old children.

Research Objectives
(a) Analyse the views of a sample of children, teachers and parents about statutory testing. (b) Consider children's parents' and teachers' views about the appropriateness of assessing children from an early age.
c) Relate the views of children, parents and teachers to theoretical concepts of childhood.

Methodology
Sample/Participants
I have decided to carry out my research project with 6 12-year-old pupils 6 parents, and 6 teachers who have had experience of teaching in preparation for the statutory tests at 11? The groups will be balanced for gender [and ethnicity?]. They will also be unrelated groups so that I can collate a variation of individual perspectives on this subject.
Access
I have good communication links with my old high school so if my research topic is approved I should be able to use this school to talk to the pupils of the sample group.
As I only want to gather general opinions from teacher's viewpoints, I will also speak to some of the teachers at this school. The remainder of my participants will come from a primary school with which I carried out a pre-teaching

course. These teachers will be especially useful, as they have had first-hand experience of educating children of this age towards the statutory tests at 11-years-old This bit needs reworking – which primary schools will you use?
I have easy access to many parents in my local area as I regularly baby-sit for some children, and I can interview the parents of my friends – two of which I understand to have a teaching background.

Timetable[included in this draft but to avoid repetition only shown below in draft three]

Data Collection Methods
I wish to carry out individual informal interviews with the children in my sample group to gather their own opinions about statutory tests, and the effects that they may have had. I will also include a brainstorming discussion with the whole of this group about various definitions of statutory tests. This will be useful as they can bounce their ideas of each other, and I will gain a more in-depth insight into their true thoughts.
I would also like to give each child a questionnaire to complete using multiple choice and open-ended questions. I think these will be useful as the pupils may find it easier to express their comments and ideas about a certain aspect of the assessment process, rather than if I was to talk to them face-to-face.
When researching the opinions of the adults involved in this study I wish to interview them separately to gain a different perspective on statutory tests. I will include what they believe to be the possible effects on themselves – depending on what viewpoint they take – children, and the concept of "childhood".

Ethical Considerations
Before completing the collection of this data, I will ensure that each participant is fully aware that the information given to me will be kept strictly confidential, and my study will not be used as a public document. They must also have signed a consent or assent form to show that they understand the aims of my research, and know that they have permission to leave the study process at any time. My target group has been chosen so as not to discriminate against any individual, with an equal number of male and female participants, and a broad variation of ages.

Deleted: and media

Deleted: well

Deleted: -

Deleted: To identify and discuss the opinions of 12-year-old children who have experienced the implications of early exams in their education, and to associate these findings to the impact made on the concept of "childhood".

Deleted: To gather and analyse the views of 12-year-old children who have completed statutory tests, and collate general opinions from teachers and parents on whether they agree with assessing children from an early age. ¶

Deleted: To examine the impact of these exams upon children teachers parents and the concept of "childhood".

Deleted: and 6 parents

Deleted: These groups will represent an equal number of both sexes and a broad variety of ages so as not to discriminate against any participant ¶

Deleted: .

FIGURE 4.1   Student research proposal example showing tutor suggestions with 'Track Changes'

KEY FACT

The word-processor function *Track Changes* allows any changes to a document to be shown in a different colour. It is particularly useful for writers who are collaborating. Once the changes have been seen, the function can be turned off and the text then shows the changed version.

The final draft which was used as the plan for the research is given below.

Final draft

Title of research: The impact of statutory tests upon young people, parents and teachers, and the concept of childhood.

Research question(s)

1 Does the target group agree with the recent literature suggesting that there is more pressure on young people nowadays to achieve academically in exams?
2 What effects do statutory tests have upon the children and their teachers?

Aim

To identify and discuss the implications of statutory testing on 12-year-old children.

Research objectives

1 To gather and analyse the views of a sample of children, teachers and parents about statutory testing.
2 To consider these views in relation to the appropriateness of assessing children from an early age.
3 To relate the views of children, parents and teachers to theoretical concepts of childhood.

Methodology

Sample/Participants

The sample will consist of six pupils, six parents and six teachers who have had experience of teaching in preparation for the statutory tests at 11. These groups will

(Continued)

(Continued)

represent an equal balance of gender, ethnicity, and a broad variety of ages so as not to discriminate against any participant.

They will also be unrelated groups so that I can collate a variety of individual perspectives on this subject.

Access

I have good communication links with my old high school so if my research topic is approved I should be able to use this school to talk to the pupils of the sample group.

As I only want to gather general opinions from teachers' viewpoints, I will also speak to some of the teachers at this school. The remainder of my participants will come from a local primary school with which I carried out a pre-teaching course. These teachers will be especially useful, as they have had first-hand experience of educating children of this age towards the statutory tests at 11 years old.

I have easy access to many parents in my local area as I regularly baby-sit for some children, and I can interview the parents of my friends – two of which I understand to have a teaching background.

Timetable

Timetable of independent study process

DATE	ACTIVITY/RESEARCH TO BE UNDERTAKEN
Semester 1	
Week 4	Draft proposal. Have first meeting with personal tutor.
Week 5	Finish typing up proposal. Do rough drafts of outline interviews and questionnaires.
Week 6	Complete ethics form, outline of interviews and questionnaires. Alter consent and assent forms and letter of introduction. Hand in proposal to office.
Week 7	Write to schools and participants asking for permission to carry out research study if approved by the ethics committee.
Weeks 8–11	Collect relevant sources in the form of books, journals, website addresses and newspaper/magazine articles to make reference to in dissertation.
Week 12	Decision from ethics committee is finalised. Make contact with personal tutor to check progress, and, if approved, collect more relevant information.
Week 13	Make first visit to school – carry out interviews and group discussion with pupils. Hand out questionnaires for them to complete.

(Continued)

(Continued)

Weeks 14 and 15	Contact personal tutor to discuss findings. Begin to analyse pupils' responses to the interviews/questionnaires in relation to the references gathered.
CHRISTMAS BREAK	Carry out interviews with parents. Make second visit to high school sometime in January to talk to some of the teachers about their opinions on the subject. Start analysis of these findings.

Semester 2

Week 1	Make contact with primary school, and carry out visit to speak to a few of the teachers about their experiences of statutory tests, from a teacher's perspective. Talk to personal tutor about findings.
Weeks 2–4	Complete analysis of all responses to interviews and questionnaires in relation to academic texts gathered.
	Make contact with tutor to check progress.
Weeks 5–7	More data collection from references to validate research study.
Week 8	Begin write-up of dissertation. Contact personal tutor to make sure I'm on the right track and discuss any problems which may have arisen.
EASTER BREAK	Complete introduction and part of the main bulk of the study. Aim to write approx. 5000–6000 words.
Week 9	Make contact with tutor to discuss what I have completed so far. Continue with write-up.
Weeks 10–11	Complete writing up the dissertation, including conclusion, bibliography, reference list, contents page and appendix. Make contact with personal tutor to discuss progress, and any problems.
Week 12	Proofreading, grammar and spell checks of dissertation, bind together and hand in on 7 May before midday!

Data collection methods

I wish to carry out individual informal interviews with the children in my sample group to gather their own opinions about statutory tests, and the effects that they may have had. I will also include a brainstorming discussion with the whole of this group about various definitions of statutory tests. This will be useful as they can bounce their ideas off each other, and I will gain a more in-depth insight into their true thoughts.

I would also like to give each child a questionnaire to complete using multiple choice and open-ended questions. I think these will be useful as the pupils may find it easier to express their comments and ideas about a certain aspect of the assessment process, rather than if I was to talk to them face to face.

(Continued)

(Continued)

When researching the opinions of the adults involved in this study I wish to interview them separately to gain a different perspective on statutory tests. I will include what they believe to be the possible effects on themselves – depending on what viewpoint they take – children, and the concept of 'childhood'.

Ethical considerations

Before completing the collection of this data, I will ensure that each participant is fully aware that the information given to me will be kept strictly confidential, and my study will not be used as a public document. They must also have signed a consent or assent form to show that they understand the aims of my research, and know that they have permission to leave the study process at any time. My target group has been chosen so as not to discriminate against any individual, with an equal number of male and female participants, and a broad variation of ages.

David carried out a good piece of research and was awarded a BA (Hons) Childhood Studies, class 2.1, for his final degree, the dissertation counting strongly towards this. He took up a place on a postgraduate teacher-training course.

DOS AND DON'TS

✓ Do

- plan your research carefully because this can avoid many problems later on
- read basic research methods texts to familiarise yourself with the research process
- think carefully about the ethics of working with children

✗ Don't

- forget the importance of a realistic timetable for your research
- worry if, after careful planning, the research doesn't go exactly to plan
- underestimate the time required for analysis of data

5

Referencing

Referencing is an important part of any academic text. This chapter explains how to reference using a particular *author/date system* ⓖ of referencing. The chapter also includes a brief explanation of the notes system. Citations and references are defined and you are shown how to set out the most common kinds of references in educational texts. The chapter concludes with some notes about software packages that can help.

There are many different systems of referencing. For example, subjects in the humanities, such as English literature and history, tend to use the notes/bibliography system. This is where you see a small (or *superscript*) number near a word. At the bottom of the page (or sometimes at the end of the book or article), the number will appear again next to a note, which often adds further explanation. Most education texts use the *Harvard* or *author/date system*. Unfortunately, the description 'Harvard system' can lead to confusion because Harvard is not one system but more a general description of a range of similar author/date referencing styles. For example, many publishers of educational books claim to use the Harvard system but their specific guidance differs. This is also true of many education journals. 'Author/date system' is a more helpful description, which means that citations feature the author's surname followed by the year of publication.

University libraries also offer guidance to students on referencing but this often explains the different kinds of systems that exist in the university rather than suggesting a style that you should follow. Most course handbooks also give guidance but you are sometimes left with more questions than answers.

The most important point is that whatever system you use, you must use it consistently. The easiest way to do that is to follow a system where the conventions are clearly laid down. In this chapter, I will show you how to use a simplified version of an author/date system explained in the *Publication Manual of the American Psychological Association: Sixth Edition (nicknamed APA 6th)*ⓖ. The reason I have chosen this is partly because many of the top journals use this style. It is also very comprehensively explained in the APA sixth book, which provides a clear set of conventions. This is important because a great deal of time and energy can be wasted on arguing about the location of things like a semicolon in a reference rather than getting on with the business of writing. The other reason that the APA 6th style is growing in influence in education is the convenient link with computer packages that help with referencing – more about that later in this chapter.

As you saw in Chapter 1, wide reading is the surest way to learn more and to achieve higher marks in your assessments. One part of this is the ability to methodically record the things that you have read and demonstrate this to the reader through your citations and reference list. A common question asked by many students is, how many references should I include in an assignment? In simple terms, the more the better, because this shows how much reading you have done. However, there's a bit more to it than that. An assessor can learn a lot from the *quality* of your references, not just the number of them. In Chapter 1, you learned about the way in which a text on an internet site differs from a book, which differs from a peer-reviewed journal article. An assignment might have a relatively small number of references but all from high-level peer-reviewed journals. If you demonstrated, through the way that you cited these texts, that you had clearly understood the articles and were able to use them effectively to enhance your writing, then this would show evidence of a higher level of learning than if you had relied mainly on internet sites. In this case, your shorter reference list would be more impressive than a longer one with lower-level publications listed.

Referencing is the process of referring to texts and ensuring that the reader has the necessary information to locate them. There are two main systems: (a) text citations and reference list (commonly called the author/date system); and (b) notes and bibliography. The main emphasis in this book is the author/date system because it is the one that is most often used in education and the social sciences. However, this chapter also gives a brief explanation of the notes/bibliography system because many education students will read publications that use this style.

The author/date system

A reference consists of two parts:

1 The citation. This is included as part of a sentence in a text: it is signalled by an author's surname and the year of publication of their text, for example (Wyse, 2005). A citation may or may not include a direct quote.
2 The entry in the reference list. The full details of the citation are given in a list at the end of the text, providing all that is required for a reader to locate and read the cited texts themselves.

⚷ KEY FACT

A reference list is an alphabetical list of full reference information about the texts that you have cited.

⚷ KEY FACT

A *bibliography* is not the same as a reference list. A bibliography includes texts that you have read but not cited.

You can look at referencing in two ways: as a rather boring convention which must be correct in an assignment, or as a vital aspect which is part of the line of argument in any assignment.

It is true that, at first glance, referencing does not appear to be a terribly sexy topic. However, if you can master referencing you will have a much stronger knowledge of academic writing and will write better assignments. I should add a third way to look at referencing – something that will stop you being thrown off your course! A full understanding of how to reference accurately, and why it is important, will ensure that you do not inadvertently *plagiarise* (see below).

The most difficult part of referencing is getting the reference list correct. Unfortunately, it is often one of the last things that you do when preparing an assignment. You may well be tired and up against a deadline, and it is at times like this when mistakes are often made. However, as I've explained, if you really check carefully, there are benefits to getting the reference list correct for the assignment as a whole, not just for reasons of conventional correctness.

The reference list should have all items arranged alphabetically at the end of the text, formatted with hanging indents (as opposed to first-line indents) and no line spaces, unless the whole text is more than single-spaced. Do not have separate sections for books and journals, and so on. Most of the examples of how to lay out citations and references in this chapter are included in the following example of a reference list (also see the layout of the reference list at the end of this book).

An example of a reference list

Adamson, A., & Jenson, V. (Writers). (2001). Shrek [Motion Picture]. In A. Warner, J. H. Williams & J. Katzenberg (Producers). United States: DreamWorks.

Alexander, R. J., Rose, J., & Woodhead, C. (1992). Curriculum Organisation and Classroom Practice in Primary Schools: A Discussion Paper [The Three Wise Men Report]. London: Department for Education and Science (DES).

American Psychological Association. (2009). *Publication Manual of the American Psychological Association* (sixth ed.). Washington, DC: American Psychological Association.

Baddeley, G. (Writer). (1992). Learning Together Through Talk: Key Stages 1 and 2 [Videocassette]. In Oracy Video (Producer). London: Hodder and Stoughton.

Harste, J. C., Woodward, V. A., & Burke, C. L. (1984). *Language Stories & Literacy Lessons*. Portsmouth, NH: Heinemann Educational Books.

Richards, C. (1997, 24 January). Individuality, equality and discovery. *Times Educational Supplement*. Retrieved from http://www.tes.co.uk/teaching-resource/Individuality-equality-and-discovery-57110/

The Scottish Government and Education Scotland. (2011). Curriculum for Excellence. Retrieved from http://www.ltscotland.org.uk/

Tizzard, B. (1993). Early influences on literacy. In R. Beard (Ed.), *Teaching Literacy Balancing Perspectives*. London: Hodder and Stoughton.

Wyse, D., Nikolajeva, M., Charlton, E., Cliff Hodges, G., Pointon, P., & Taylor, L. (2011). Place-related identity, texts, and transcultural meanings. *British Educational Research Journal*. doi: 10.1080/01411926.2011.608251

★ TOP TIP

Do not include texts that you have read but have not cited in your assignment. You only do this if the assignment has a bibliography rather than a reference list.

KEY FACT

The use of too many direct quotes is often a sign of weak writing.

The sections below illustrate a simplified version of the APA 6th referencing style (American Psychological Association, 2009). It shows you exactly how to correctly reference the most commonly used sources in assignments in education and the social sciences.

How to lay out citations and references

Book

Example of citation:

> Harste, Woodward & Burke (1984) investigated the language and literacy experiences of 68 children aged between three and six. Their evidence strongly emphasised the positive achievements of these children. The conclusions of the study raised some challenging questions about nursery teachers' expectations of children.

Entry in reference list:

Harste, J. C., Woodward, V. A., & Burke, C. L. (1984). *Language Stories & Literacy Lessons*. Portsmouth, NH: Heinemann Educational Books.

When a text has two authors, always cite both names. When a text has three, four or five authors, cite all authors the first time. In subsequent citations, use the surname of the first author followed by et al. 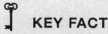 (not in italics) and the year of publication. When a text has six or more authors, cite the name of the first author followed by 'et al.'. All authors' names should appear in the reference list unless there are more than seven names; then you should provide the initials and surnames of the first six authors followed by an ellipsis (...) to replace some authors' names, then the final author's name.

KEY FACT

'Et al.' literally means 'and others'.

The actual year of publication should be used, *not* reprint dates. If the book is a second edition then the edition date is used and the title in the reference list will include the words *2nd edition* (or *3rd edition* and so on).

Chapter in an edited book

Citation:
Wyse & Opfer (2010) identified politicians' perception of risk as a factor in a decline in trust in professionals.

Reference:
Wyse, D., & Opfer, D. (2010). Globalisation and the international context for literacy policy reform in England. In D. Wyse, R. Andrews & J. Hoffman (Eds.), *The Routledge International Handbook of English, Language and Literacy Teaching.* London: Routledge. pp. 438–447.

Citation:
Tizard (1993) found that early learning of the alphabet and children's skill at writing their names were indicators of future reading achievement. She pointed out that although there were other indicators her research was unable to verify that they had the same influence.

Reference:
Tizard, B. (1993). Early influences on literacy. In R. Beard (Ed.), *Teaching Literacy: Balancing Perspectives.* London: Hodder and Stoughton.

Notice that the normal order for surname and initial is reversed for the editor's name, for whom the initial is first.

Journal article – in printed form

Citation:
Wyse (2003) showed that the National Literacy Strategy Framework for Teaching was not adequately supported by research evidence.

Reference:
Wyse, D. (2003). The National Literacy Strategy: A critical review of empirical evidence. *British Educational Research Journal,* 29(6): 903–916.

You need the volume, the issue number in brackets (if there is one) and the page range from the first to last page of the article.

Electronic formats

Increasingly, sources that you cite will be electronic ones. A relatively new development is the inclusion of the DOI (digital object identifier) number for electronic sources. If this number is present, you should use it: see 'Journal article – in electronic form' example below. If a doi is not present then use the web address: see the example under 'Organisation as author – in electronic form (website)' below.

Journal article – in electronic form

Citation:
Wyse et al. (2011) proposed the theory of *transcultural meanings* to explain place-related identity.

Reference:
Wyse, D., Nikolajeva, M., Charlton, E., Cliff Hodges, G., Pointon, P., & Taylor, L. (2011). Place-related identity, texts, and transcultural meanings. *British Educational Research Journal*. Advance online publication. doi: 10.1080/01411926.2011.608251

If the volume number and issue number are available then insert them in the same format as the printed form. When journal articles are released online in advance, they sometimes don't have a volume and issue at first.

Organisation as author – in electronic form (website)

Citation:
Scotland's Curriculum for Excellence (The Scottish Government and Education Scotland, 2011) was developed following the devolution of the countries of the UK from England.

Reference:
The Scottish Government and Education Scotland. (2011). Curriculum for Excellence. Retrieved from http://www.ltscotland.org.uk/

Organisation as author – school policy document

Citation:
The school policy on language (Beverley Primary School, 2012) was exemplary because the school is in Yorkshire!

Reference:
Beverley Primary School. (2012). Language for Life: Why Literacy is not the only Fruit. Beverley: Beverley Primary School.

Newspaper – in electronic form without DOI (website)

Citation:
The continuing interest in the Plowden Report was revealed by a special section in the *Times Educational Supplement*, which included an important article by Richards (1997).

Reference:
Richards, C. (1997, 24 January). Individuality, equality and discovery. *Times Educational Supplement*. Retrieved from http://www.tes.co.uk/teaching-resource/Individuality-equality-and-discovery-57110/

Newspaper – in printed form

Reference:
Adams, T. (2011, 16 October). Nights with a duchess – and a tricky first novel. *The Observer*. p. 3.

Newspapers should not be used to strengthen your argument in the way that books and journals can. However, they can be used if your focus is to analyse the way that the media writes about things and to give an indication of the current events of the time.

Report

Citation:
Alexander, Rose & Woodhead (1992) were critical of a number of aspects of primary education including the practice of the integrated day, which was also known as 'topic work'.

Reference:
Alexander, R. J., Rose, J., & Woodhead, C. (1992). Curriculum Organisation and Classroom Practice in Primary Schools: A Discussion Paper [The Three Wise Men Report]. London: Department for Education and Science (DES).

The information in square brackets is not part of the reference but may help readers who are more familiar with the alternative name. Government departments often change their name (for example, DES, DfE, DfEE, DfES) so make sure that you have the correct version.

 KEY FACT

Square brackets are used to indicate that you have added some information that is not part of a text that you are referring to.

Film/video

Citation:
The humorous way that Shrek (Adamson & Jenson, 2001) satirises classic Disney films is at its height in the scene with the exploding bird duet.

Reference:
Adamson, A., & Jenson, V. (Writers). (2001). Shrek [Motion Picture]. In A. Warner, J. H. Williams & J. Katzenberg (Producers). Glendale, CA: DreamWorks Animation.

Citation:
The Baddeley (1992) video supports the pack by showing good practice in speaking and listening.

Reference:
Baddeley, G. (Writer). (1992). Learning Together Through Talk: Key Stages 1 and 2 [Videocassette]. In Oracy Video (Producer). London: Hodder and Stoughton.

Secondary source

Citation:
In relation to the teaching of reading, the phrase 'the great debate' has been attributed to Chall (as cited in Wray & Medwell, 1994).

Reference:
Wray, D., & Medwell, J. (1994). *Teaching Primary English: The State of the Art*. London: Routledge.

If you cite a text cited by someone else, it is known as a secondary source. You should give the secondary source in the reference list. In the main text, name the original work and cite the secondary source. Use the author of the original text but in brackets put 'as cited in …' followed by the author(s) of the secondary source.

Do not use secondary sources unless the text is very important to your argument and it is not possible to get an inter-library loan. You should read texts yourself first hand because the author of the secondary source may have misread the text and is likely to interpret it in a different way from yourself. You learn more by reading things yourself.

You could also be accused of plagiarism if it appears from your citations and references that you read several primary sources, but in fact had only read secondary sources and did not cite your secondary sources, as shown here.

Conference presentation

Citation:
Sir Jim Rose, who led the Rose Review, put forward his controversial rationale for recommending that synthetic phonics should be imposed on all schools (Rose, 2006).

Reference:
Rose, J. (2006, 8 July). *Review of Early Reading*. Paper presented at the After 'Rose', Which Way Forward? One Day Conference, Roehampton, University Kairos Conference Centre.

Lecture

This reference format is probably the most appropriate if you want to cite something from one of your lectures:

Wyse, D. (2005, 18 November). Spelling. Lecture presented as part of PGCE Early Years and Primary Education Course, University of Cambridge.

Laws

You do not need to include laws in your reference list; they are usually only cited in the main text. You should always include the year of the law (not in brackets) after its name.

> Kenneth Baker was the education minister when the Educational Reform Act 1988 was enacted.

Classic texts

Citation:
You can see evidence of Carroll's work as a mathematician in his classic text Alice in Wonderland (Carroll, 1863).

Reference:
Carroll, L. (1984). *Alice's Adventures in Wonderland*. London: Gollanz. (Original work published 1863)

The reference should show both the original date of publication and the date of the version that you read.

Quotes: long, short, and quotation marks

The best academic writing uses quotations sparingly. In the early stages of learning to write academically, there can be a tendency to hide behind the words of others. In addition to a natural lack of confidence in your own ideas, this can sometimes represent a lack of understanding. For example, rather than put the idea into your own words as part of your own argument, you insert a quote just to show that you have read something! If your reading, recording and transforming of ideas into your own line of argument is good, then you will tend to paraphrase and cite key ideas and authors more than quote directly.

If you do need a quotation then the main reason should be that it is particularly important to your argument and you want to emphasise that the author of the quote has something really significant to say. It should also be a quote that you spend some time discussing as part of your writing. Notice that a long quote of 40 or more words should be indented, with author, date and page number placed either in the introductory text or immediately following the quote. You do not need quotation marks for a quote of this kind.

Here's what the above paragraph would look like when laid out as a long quote:

> If you do need a quotation then the main reason should be that it is particularly important to your argument and you want to emphasise that the author of the quote has something really significant to say. It should also be a quote that you spend some time discussing as part of your writing. Notice that a long quote of 40 or more words should be indented, with author, date and page number

placed either in the introductory text or immediately following the quote. You do not need quotation marks for a quote of this kind. (Wyse, 2012, p. 64)

A quote of less than 40 words should have double quotation marks and should not be indented because it is integrated within the grammar of the sentence. Single quotation marks are used for quotes within quotes. Single quote marks are also used for direct speech and turns of phrase.

KEY FACT

The grammar of the sentence which includes the quote should make complete sense and should flow appropriately.

★ TOP TIP

Do not have too many quotes of more than 40 words. One or two in a 3500-word assignment is usually enough.

If you notice too many direct quotes, you may find that the draft of your writing should be viewed as an early version rather than as a final draft. Go back to the texts that you are citing and read them again. Follow the advice offered in this book on critical reading and systematic recording (Chapter 2).

The notes/bibliography system

Some people studying education engage with texts based in the arts, humanities, history and philosophy. These texts often provide the reader with reference information in the form of notes and a bibliography. There are several main types of notes/bibliography systems, but in this book I introduce you to one of the most user-friendly versions.

The main difference from the author/date system is that in the main text a note number is used instead of the author's name and year of publication for the citation. In the notes/bibliography system, the main text is not cluttered up with surnames, years and brackets because instead there are just small (or superscript) numbers. However, the footnotes, endnotes (or both) can become very complicated indeed. This is not least because of the need to sometimes use abbreviations such as *ibid.* ⒢ (in full *ibidem*, which means 'in the same place') or *op. cit.* ⒢ (*opere citato*, 'in the work already cited') in order to refer back to previous notes.

The example of an extract of text formatted using the notes and bibliography system is on the next page. The footnote numbers are generated automatically by a function in the word processor's insert menu. A shortened form of the bibliographic information is included in the footnote. This is simply the surname, the first few words from the title, and indication of the specific point in the cited text, such as a page number. The entry in the bibliography that corresponds with the information in the footnote has the full publication information, but you can see that the year of publication appears at the end, unlike in the author/date system.

An example of text using the notes/bibliography system

Logical value to Dewey was curriculum organisation that represented the best knowledge in society organised through a natural progression involving authentic hands-on experiences for the child. He said, 'Guidance [by educators] is not external imposition. *It is freeing the life-process for its own most adequate fulfilment.*' [italics in original][1]

Too often educators make assumptions about children's experiences and ideas; consequently there can be a disparity between home settings and formal educational settings[2]. To a certain extent this disparity is natural as formal educational settings are, as the phrase suggests, formal. But there is much that educators can do to recognise and build on children's home experiences. One aspect is a particular state of mind rather than direct action. This is an open mind about children's home experiences, an awareness that deficit models and low expectations of children impact negatively on learning, and a genuine interest to understand the positive features of children's experiences out of school.

---

[1]Dewey, *The Child and the Curriculum*, 17.
[2]Wells, *The Meaning Makers*.

Bibliography [this would normally be at the end of the book]

Dewey, J. *The Child and the Curriculum*. Chicago: The University of Chicago Press, 1902.

Wells, G. *The Meaning Makers: Children Learning Language and Using Language to Learn.* London: Hodder and Stoughton, 1986.

The notes/bibliography system is comprehensively covered in a book called *The Chicago Manual of Style* (a quick guide is provided at http://www.chicagomanualofstyle.org/).

Software to help with citations and references

As you can see, it is not an easy task to create a perfect set of citations and references. However, further help is at hand. Various computer packages will do it all for you. Hmm, if only it was as simple as that. *EndNote* is a good popular referencing package that I discuss below, although it is expensive if you have to buy it yourself. *Zotero* (http://www.zotero.org/), on the other hand, is a free online tool that has many of the features of EndNote. MS Word has some automatic referencing facilities, but they are rather primitive compared to these other packages.

It is true that EndNote can make the task of citing and referencing much easier. In order to use it, though, you need to be sure that you understand the principles of referencing that have been outlined in this chapter. Then you will need to familiarise yourself with the way that the software works. Finally, you should try to use EndNote as part of your work for an assignment and learn more about how it works, by using it.

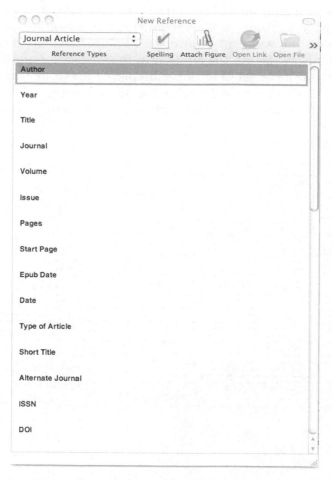

FIGURE 5.1   EndNote software New Record window

Any references that you find have to be entered into what is called the EndNote 'library'. This is a complete list of all the references that you have entered. There are two main ways to enter references. The simplest way is to use the 'new record' function, as shown in Figure 5.1. You complete the relevant categories for the kind of reference that you are entering and then as soon as the window is closed, the reference is added to the library.

Another way of entering references can save you considerable amounts of time. If you have done a search on the British Education Index (see Chapter 2), you can import the references directly in the style that they were saved in the index so you do not even need to type them yourself.

After you have entered the references, the EndNote library looks like Figure 5.2.

Having built up your EndNote library of references, it is very straight-forward to insert a citation and reference into your text. You select the reference in the EndNote library and then position the cursor at the place in your document where you want the citation to be placed. When you click the relevant icon, EndNote inserts the citation in the correct format (depending on which format you have selected, for example APA 6th or Chicago 16th). If there is more than one citation with the same name and year, EndNote automatically adds the appropriate letters, for example (Wyse, 2005a), to

FIGURE 5.2   EndNote library window

demarcate the different references. Finally, EndNote inserts the full reference in the correct place in the reference list and in the correct format. The other possibility is to use the 'copy formatted' function, which is more like a normal copy-and-paste action.

If you do not use a package like EndNote then you will need to methodically go through your writing to check all your references. The best way to do this is to print out a copy of your references and then tick them off as you come to each citation in the main text. Remember that, as well as checking for missing references, you may find some extras that you thought you would use but then didn't cite in the final draft. These will need deleting.

Plagiarism

Plagiarism is "the unacknowledged use of the work of others as if this were your own original work" (University of Cambridge Board of Graduate Studies, 2007, online). It is most serious when there has been an intention to deceive in order to gain unfair advantage. The penalties for students who plagiarise are failed assessments and the ultimate sanction of being thrown off the course. However, quite apart from the dishonesty that is involved, there is a contradiction with the idea that studying should be enjoyable, and that a natural part of studying is the process of acknowledging the work of more experienced people in a field. It is a real pleasure to read something that makes us think differently or something that helps bring ideas into sharp focus. The need to acknowledge other people's work is also a matter of academic integrity. Imagine how you feel when you help somebody and they don't even acknowledge what you have done, or, worse still, they say, 'well, I didn't ask you to do that'! Plagiarism shows a lack of respect for people and their work.

The most sloppy form of plagiarism is simply cutting and pasting from the internet and pretending the work is your own. Fortunately, there is a range of software designed to detect such cheating, for example CopyCatch.com, Eve, Findsome.com, Turnitin.com and Wordcheck. Some students inadvertently plagiarise because they are not systematic about recording what they have read, so they forget which are their own words and which are the words of published authors. Unfortunately, this is not seen as a reasonable excuse, so if you inadvertently plagiarise you will be penalised.

The University of Cambridge defines plagiarism as follows:

> Candidates are advised that plagiarism can be defined as: the unacknowledged use of the work of others as if this were your own original work. In the context of an examination, this amounts to a candidate passing off

the work of others as his/her own to gain unfair advantage. Examiners must be left in no doubt as to which parts of the work are the candidate's own and which are the rightful property of someone else.

The guidance goes on to say:

Plagiarism may be due to:

Copying (using another person's language and/or ideas as if they are your own);

Collusion (where collaboration is concealed or has been expressly forbidden, in order to gain unfair advantage)

Methods include:

quoting directly another person's language, data or illustrations without clear indication that the authorship is not your own and due acknowledgement of the source;

paraphrasing the critical work of others without due acknowledgement – even if you change some words or the order of the words, this is still plagiarism if you are using someone else's original ideas and are not properly acknowledging it;

using ideas taken from someone else without reference to the originator;

cutting and pasting from the Internet to make a 'pastiche' of online sources;

colluding with another person, including another candidate (other than as might be permitted for joint project work);

submitting as part of your own report or dissertation someone else's work without identifying clearly who did the work (for example, where research has been contributed by others to a joint project) or submitting work that has been undertaken in whole or in part by someone else on your behalf (such as employing a 'ghost writing service');

submitting work you have submitted for a qualification at another institution without declaring it and clearly indicating the extent of overlap;

deliberately reproducing someone else's work in a written examination.

Plagiarism can occur in respect to all types of sources and all media:

not just text, but also illustrations, musical quotations, computer code etc.;

not just text published in books and journals, but also downloaded from websites or drawn from other media;

not just published material but also unpublished works, including lecture hand-outs and the work of other students. (University of Cambridge Board of Graduate Studies, 2007, online)

The most difficult point in the list above is the idea that even if you change someone else's words, this would still be regarded as plagiarism if you did not accurately *cite* (see above) their work. You might be wondering how you can fairly use other people's work but avoid being accused of plagiarism. Two ideas will help here:

1 Although you will read other people's work, critically evaluate it, and in the process be influenced by it, you should always clearly put forward your own points of view throughout an assignment.
2 Remember that giving proper recognition of other people's work is a strength in your writing, not a weakness.

The best way to avoid plagiarism is to engage fully with your learning, including developing your own clear ideas about issues in education. Critically evaluate and synthesise a range of texts in order to confidently put forward your own lines of argument. Finally, ensure that you reference correctly.

DOS AND DON'TS

✓ Do

- systematically record information and ideas as part of your background reading
- use the conventions explained in this chapter
- check that in your final draft the citations match the entries in your reference list, and that there aren't any extra references that in the end you did not cite

✗ Don't

- regard referencing as insignificant
- mix different styles of referencing
- paraphrase other people's texts (including those on the internet) without a proper citation and reference

Part II

Writing

6

Structuring Your Writing

After reading this chapter, you will understand better how to structure academic writing. You will know about the typical sections to include in a dissertation and their word lengths. You will be able to use this information to support the writing of other assignments.

The overall structure of a piece of writing is reflected in the following elements:

- the title
- the contents page, including the organisation of chapters (if the text is long enough to require this)
- subheadings and sections
- paragraphs
- general layout features
- the number of words overall, and in different sections.

The number of words in a text is one important feature of the structure. It is possible to write about a topic in 100 words, 1000 words, 10,000 words or 100,000 words. A piece of 100,000 words is book length and requires chapters. A piece of 100 words is abstract length (like the summary paragraph at the beginning of this chapter) and may or may not even require paragraphs.

 KEY FACT

One page of text at font size 12 is about 500 words. If it is double-spaced then two pages equal 500 words.

You might think that the first thing that should be written is the title but this is not always the case. The title needs to sum up succinctly, and at times imaginatively, the whole text, but this can be quite difficult to decide until the whole text has been written. This raises the question of what happens when you begin a piece of writing.

★ **TOP TIP**

Leave the title until you've finished writing the whole text.

Student example: beginning your writing

Jim had started drafting a 12,000-word document in support of his proposal for the PhD research he wanted to carry out. The focus of the proposed research was creativity in primary education. The first sentence of the document was as follows: "In the age of knowledge economy, economic growth, a feature of scientific and technological revolutions, correlates with innovation potential."

A narrow evaluation of this sentence might simply be to say that the grammar of the first phrase is non-standard and should be: 'In the age of the knowledge economy ...'. Although this is a necessary correction, on its own it would be narrow evaluation because of the neglect of a myriad of arguably more important considerations. For example, there is the question of whether the knowledge economy can legitimately be described as 'an age'. Evaluation of the phrase also means appreciating its role as part of the meaning of the sentence as a whole. The sentence had a particular importance because of its location as the first sentence of the first paragraph of the text. The first word, sentence, paragraph, page, chapter, determine the overall character of the text, and are the things that readers are particularly sensitive to. In addition, the student's sentence served as a topic sentence for the paragraph.

The paragraph went on to make the case that creativity is a major component of 'innovation potential' and that there is a relationship between creativity and national competitiveness. So the topic sentence was not a sufficiently coherent indicator for what was to follow. Finally, there was the question of whether the topic of the knowledge economy was the most appropriate for the start of the document. The answer to this included consideration of genre, audience and the academic discipline of education where the student's work was located. It was suggested by Jim's tutor that the second paragraph that summarised the importance of creativity for human civilisation was a more appropriate beginning to the piece because of the 'bigger picture' that the topic of human civilisation portrayed. The tutor had the view that a sequence of ideas that progressed from the overarching idea about human civilisation to the important but more narrowly focused idea of creativity and innovation might be a more appropriate sequence.

Although beginnings are often tricky, it is better to try and write something, almost anything, because once some words are down on the page they can be edited in the ways that the example above suggests.

Student example: beginnings, structure, sections and paragraphs

Jean's assignment was to write a 500-word report about some observations that she had made of two children while on school placement. The structure of her first draft is shown in Table 6.1.

As I've said, the first sentence and paragraph of any piece of work are very important because the reader quickly forms judgements about your writing at the beginning. Jean's idea to explain the way that the observations were carried out was a good one, although she might have improved this with a previous introductory paragraph about some published classroom observation work that she had read. Even in a very short piece like this, you can see that the idea of literature review is relevant, even if it is only one paragraph.

The phrase "For this assignment" was a weak start because it did not positively signal what the paragraph was about. It also sounded as though it was the kind of sentence that you might have halfway through a paragraph rather than at the beginning. A more direct opening sentence might have been: 'During my first placement I recorded observations of two children in the Year 1 class where I was working. The observations were carried out for 10 minutes per day.' The topic of the first paragraph has now clearly been signalled as information about the process carried out for the assignment.

TABLE 6.1   The structure of the opening of the first draft of Jean's assignment

Paragraph	Topic of paragraph	First (topic) sentence
1	Information about observation process	"For this assignment we had to carry out on-going observations of two different children ..."
2	Age of children; characteristics of Child A; characteristics of Child B	"The children who were being observed were in Year 1, age five."
3	Target-setting	"For this assignment, targets were set with the class teacher ..."

The topic sentence in paragraph two would then have become redundant because the information would have been moved to paragraph one. As it happened, the second sentence of paragraph two made a better topic sentence: "Child A talked a lot during her work", although we might have wanted a more general phrase about the child overall before getting down to detail: 'Child A was more extrovert than the other children in the group, which was evident from the amount of talk that she did while working.' With either version, it is now clear that the second paragraph is all about Child A (I prefer fictionalised names to letter or other codes because they are more natural for the reader).

You will have seen from Table 6.1 that the second paragraph originally contained at least two major topics, information about Child A and Child B. The paragraph also looked long on the page and in fact was about 200 words (which is two-fifths of the whole assignment), suggesting that it needed to be split. Halfway through the paragraph, the topic changed: 'However, Child B was very different, she was …'. This was the perfect point to split the paragraph. A better start to paragraph three would have been: 'Child B was a quiet child …'.

Paragraph four began with the same weak phrase as the opening sentence ('For this assignment …'); repetition is something that you should always be on your guard against because if used unintentionally it appears weak. The best way to improve the sentence is simply to delete the first three words of the topic sentence and use the rest: 'Targets were set with the class teacher for each of the two children.' After carrying out these changes, the structure is much improved. Jean's concluding paragraph was a good one which summarised the main things that she had learned by carrying out the work.

Despite the fact that the example was a different kind of assignment from the research report covered later in this chapter, Table 6.2 shows that there are clear links between the two forms.

TABLE 6.2   The links between the research report structure and the example of an assignment

Paragraph and links with research report structure	Topic of paragraph	First (topic) sentence
1 Methods	First practice, observations	During my first placement I recorded observations of two children in the Year 1 class where I was working. The observations were carried out for 10 minutes per day …
2 Findings	Child A	Child A had an extrovert personality, which was evident from the amount of talk that she did while working.
3 Findings	Child B	Child B was a quiet child …
4 Findings	Target-setting	Targets were set with the class teacher for each of the two children.

Subheadings and sections

Subheadings are used to divide the text into large sections. Like the title, the subheading should clearly sum up the content of the section. Too few sub-headings can make it more difficult for you to communicate the flow of your argument to the reader. Only very skilful writers can maintain clarity in long pieces without subheadings (stories are different to academic texts in this respect because the narrative of the story maintains the flow). However, too many subheadings can break the flow of your writing, which can distract the reader from your intended meaning. Remember that the marker of your writing will often be reading quickly; good use of subheadings can help readers understand your points more quickly and clearly, which can lead to a better impression.

★ TOP TIP

On average, for a 3000-word essay, try at least one subheading per 500 words.

A subheading is the title for a section; a section is built from paragraphs. Quite a lot of students struggle with paragraph structure. First of all, you need to understand what a paragraph is and how it works. A paragraph is a block of text which consists of a number of sentences about a particular topic. The first sentence of a paragraph is often referred to as the 'topic sentence' because it reveals to the reader what the topic of the paragraph is.

★ TOP TIP

It is very rare to have a paragraph of only one sentence – if you spot one, check to see if the sentence would be better joined to the paragraph before or after.

If you are using a word processor, it is a good idea to use the automatic heading *styles* for your subheadings. The reason for using these, rather than creating your own formatting for subheadings, is that the word processor recognises them and makes them part of the *document map*. The document map looks a bit like a contents page (and for long texts, word processors can actually create a contents page for you, complete with the correct page numbers). If you click on the document map icon, all the headings in your document are revealed in the left margin. If you click on any of the headings, the cursor jumps to that section of the text. The document map is very helpful because it enables you to think about the order, number and hierarchy of your headings and sections – in other words, the overall structure of your writing. The simplest hierarchy is to have the title of your writing at the level of 'heading 1' and the subheadings all at the level of 'heading 2'. If some sections are subsets of other sections then you will need to use 'heading 3', and so on. One of the biggest challenges when writing a long piece such as a dissertation is being able to keep in mind the whole structure as you write the individual sections – the document map is an invaluable aid for this provided you use the auto heading styles (you may need to configure your word processor's *normal template* to ensure that the formatting of these headings is appropriate in relation to the presentation features required by your course).

The paragraphs in a subheaded section represent a sequence of ideas that you are putting forward. They must have a logical order to them. The last sentence of one paragraph leads the reader into the topic sentence of the next paragraph. However, this flow of ideas is subtle. It is not that you need to *explicitly* make links between paragraphs. It is more that the careful placement of paragraphs and use of sentences will result in the logical order and satisfactory flow of ideas.

Writing a dissertation

Assessments which ask you to carry out observations and/or a piece of research in the classroom and then write this up are common to many courses. It is common for a course to have a final assessment like this, which is sometimes called a dissertation.

KEY FACT

A dissertation is an extended piece of formal writing which explores a topic in depth and is usually based upon original research. The term is related to the word 'discourse'.

A dissertation of this sort is basically a research report. In this chapter, I am going to concentrate on how to structure a good research report because it is one of the most challenging and important pieces of writing that you are likely to do. The structure of a research report is not the same as the structure of some other kinds of assessments such as lesson planning, presentations, evaluations, and so on. However, if you can structure a research report really well, you will find that you will also be better equipped to tackle other kinds of writing because much of the knowledge and skills can be transferred.

The purpose of a research report is to tell the reader how you carried out your research and what you found out. Often, some of the writing for the report is drafted while you are still collecting the data. This sometimes results in students mistakenly using the future tense (for example, 'I will be keeping a research diary') but the whole report should be in the past tense ('I kept a research diary') because ultimately you are reporting on something that has been done in the past, once you have finished the research.

Academic writing has a particular formal style. Every word is important so you have to use language very carefully. Avoid using language which is too informal, like the kinds of phrases that you might use when speaking. At the same time, your use of language should be direct and clear; there is no need to use complicated language or 'big words' for the sake of it.

★ TOP TIP

Avoid the kind of informal language that these students used:

Informal: "As part of our topic on insects we are going to *do the park*."
Formal: 'As part of our topic on insects we are going to visit the park.'
Informal: "The children *absolutely loved* this book."
Formal: 'The children really enjoyed *Burglar Bill*.'

You need to be careful about making claims about your research which cannot be supported by your data and their analysis. Clauses such as

'my research found some evidence that ...' or

'it is possible that ...' or

'although my findings revealed ... other studies have shown a different picture ...'

are often suitable for the discussion section because they are tentative and they show that you understand that your findings are limited to the data you acquired. Your points should be based on evidence (only from your own research data and from published research), not your personal opinions. Personal opinions are sometimes called *anecdotal evidence* **G**.

🔑 KEY FACT

Anecdotal evidence is the information that we gather in our daily lives and that informs our beliefs about the world. It is not the same as evidence that is gathered as part of research.

Some people say that you should not put forward your own point of view in a piece of academic writing. This is not accurate. A good piece of academic writing does clearly put forward the writer's view about the subject; the key thing is that the writer also considers a range of evidence that offers different perspectives to their own.

Beginning a piece of writing can often be the hardest part. Although careful planning and thinking are important, there comes a point when you must start writing. Do not worry too much about getting the words exactly right at first. You will find that much of the early draft will be changed anyway. Some students put the subheading 'Introduction' right at the beginning of their text. I would advise you not to do this. The introduction is simply the sentences and paragraphs at the beginning of your text. Yes, you have to choose opening sentences and paragraphs carefully so that they do sound like the beginning, but there is no need for a separate introduction complete with subheading (only very long texts such as books need a separate introduction of this kind).

★ TOP TIP

Start the first draft of your writing and then delete some early sentences (or even paragraphs) in favour of a sentence later on that is more appropriate to begin your piece.

A suggested structure for a dissertation or research report

There are four main sections that you would expect to see in a good research report:

1   literature review
2   methodology
3   findings/results
4   discussion.

1   Literature review – a review of texts related to your research topic

Not to be confused with book/film reviews in the media, an academic literature review is a section that gives an overview of texts in your field and shows that you have read widely about your topic. If it is written well, it also shows how your work contributes to the field, however modest this contribution may be.

- Introduce your topic of study.
- If your topic is one that is currently featured in the media, this can be a moment to link with this. In general, though, references to newspaper sources are not academically rigorous and so do not support your arguments (see Chapter 1).
- Sometimes it can help to include personal reasons for choosing the area of study, such as experiences that you had while on school experience, why you decided to do the research, or previous research that you have done. This is a rare occasion when personal comment can be appropriate. However, even in this part of the dissertation, it is tricky to get the tone right.
- Theoretical perspectives are necessary to put your dissertation into a wider context and to achieve the highest marks. Theory is difficult to define because it varies so much. Some theories are short and to the point: for example, women make better drivers than men. Other theories are long and complex.

KEY FACT

Theory can be defined as ideas which explain and summarise things. In research, theory is developed or confirmed by observation and experiment.

Most publications related to your topic will include some theory. Identify sections which emphasise theory, rather than research and/or practice, during your reading. Organise the key theoretical ideas as a basis for some paragraphs in your literature review.

- Define the key ideas and terms that you will use throughout the report by citing researchers' definitions published in articles. Be careful about standard dictionary definitions because some technical words can have a different meaning from the one used in everyday life (although dictionaries like the *Oxford English Dictionary* do include technical meanings of words). For example, the word 'genre' refers to different kinds of novels (like crime or romance) in everyday life, but in education it has been defined broadly as the structural features of any specific spoken or written act.

- Show that you are aware of the most recent research that is as closely related to your own as possible. Show that you have a wide knowledge of the field by making reference to some key older texts (seminal texts) that are still regarded as important.

Organise the literature review by using subheadings. When you read a selection of texts, you usually find that there are some key topics that keep cropping up. Choose some of these topics as the basis for the sections of your literature review.

Here is an example of subheadings from a student's children's literature essay:

Reasons for choice of Roald Dahl

Sociological aspect of children's literature
Historical events
Roald Dahl – his life
Book analyses
Other authors

2   Methodology – an account of the methods that you used and reflections on their effectiveness

A methodology section includes the ways that you think about research philosophically, the kind of research that you are undertaking, and the methods that you used. Here, you need to do three things:

1   Clearly explain the methods that you used.
2   Show a deeper level of understanding of methodology by citing research methods texts.
3   Show your awareness of the strengths and weaknesses of the methods that you used in your research. Some of this awareness can be shown by a combination of 1 and 2.

This applies to:

- Theory – there are theories about your topic but there are also theories about methodology – for example, are you collecting mainly quantitative or qualitative data? Why? The answer to the question lies in methodological theory and its link with your objectives. Once again, theoretical exploration will help you gain the highest marks.
- Research questions/aim/objectives – clear aims and objectives are vital because they should be the anchor for the whole study. Research questions *and* aims may not both be needed because they are somewhat interchangeable.

★ **TOP TIP**

Limit yourself to one aim and three objectives which link with your research questions.

- Sample and site(s) – give straightforward details about the participants in your research. The most basic and essential information is the number of people involved. A table can usefully set out the following information: fictional name, gender, age, ethnic origin. If the site is a school then the type of school (infant, primary) and information such as numbers of free school meals, numbers of minority ethnic pupils, and location (for example, inner-city, rural) are helpful. You should also explain how you were able to access the school.
- Ethics – statements about ethics have become much more important in recent years, particularly in research with children. The main aspects of this are:

  1 separate informed consent by children, parents and other participants
  2 the right to withdraw from research without prejudice
  3 confidentiality, unless there is a duty to report something (for example, a disclosure about child abuse)
  4 the extent to which the research is in the best interests of children
  5 special care when working with disadvantaged groups

- Fieldwork – a timetable showing the dates of visits, observations, interviews, and so on.
- Data-collection methods – the methods that were used to collect the data.
- Analysis – a short account of how the data were organised and analysed.
- Validity – what techniques did you use to ensure your study was valid?

In the methodology section, you should cite research methods texts, not texts about the topic of study (sometimes called the 'substantive area').

3 Findings/results – a report of the most significant things that you found

The findings section is an account of the things that you discovered as a result of your research. There is some debate about the difference between findings and analysis. Analysis is something that you do by working with your data. It is something that is done largely in the mind by working on the data. Having carried out this analysis, you should be in a position to report a series of findings. Often, students think that they have produced findings when actually their first draft represents analysis.

★ **TOP TIP**

Think of early writing drafts of the findings section as tools for analysing your data, rather than as finished writing.

Remember that you cannot have valid findings without rigorous, systematic and exhaustive analysis.

Following analysis, you must *select* the most significant findings. To do this, you need to decide which information is most important and which information you will not report. There are many possibilities for presentation:

- The use of subheadings which represent substantial categories that emerged during your analysis is often the best way to report findings.

Kathy used the following subheadings to structure her findings section. The headings had emerged as categories during the analysis of her data:

- Adult or child agendas?
- School council ideas – major and minor
- Progress on suggestions from last school council
- Management of the school council
- Councillors' views and their class's views
- Tokenism

- Case studies of particular participants and/or sites, and so on, can form the main basis of the findings or can enhance other forms of presentation.
- Chronological accounts – these may be useful if the sequence of time was an important feature of the research, perhaps if you were using a diary to track your development during a teaching practice.
- Graphical representation – many people find the use of diagrams and tables to sum up findings helpful.

★ **TOP TIP**

Tables are useful for summarising text-based data as well as numbers-based data.

- Presentation organised in order of data-collection methods. This can be too simplistic and often represents analysis more than findings, but is necessary for some findings sections, for example when reporting the outcomes of research using mixed methods designs.
- Using different written genres – this requires great confidence, and skill. Poetry and drama have been used to report research! I once presented the findings of a study about ten teachers' English teaching as a play. One of the findings of the research was that the teachers felt inhibited by the OfSTED inspection regime and most unsure about the coherence of the policies. A chief inspector was portrayed as a babbling, incoherent, drunkard character in the play in order to stimulate debate about this finding.

The findings section should not normally include citations unless the whole study is an analysis of texts. The findings are presented in your own words.

4   Discussion – the implications of the research project

The discussion section brings the line of argument in your writing to its conclusion – it is where the most important outcomes of the research are communicated. This is often a difficult section to write. However, if it proves to be extremely difficult, it may be that you have not analysed your data deeply enough. If so, go back to your analysis and findings.

Some people explicitly return to their research objectives at this point. While it is true that the whole report should be clearly related to your objectives, this often works better if it is implicit in the writing. However, the restatement of objectives and reflections on how well you met them clearly signals to the person marking the assignment that you have thought about this. The discussion section should include the following:

- Main findings – a bulleted summary perhaps.
- A short discussion about the one overall finding of the study and what you conclude from this. If space permits, a short discussion about one or more of your other main findings without repeating information in the findings section.
- Implications of your research – how might your conclusions be acted on by the participants in the study? What impact does the research have on your future thinking and practice? Can the conclusions be tentatively related to a wider perspective, such as the possible impact on practice and other people's lives, or links with the broader society?
- A revisiting of one or two key studies from the literature review, and a note about how you now view them in the light of having done your research.
- Optional reflections on limitations of the study – although this is traditional, it is often better covered within the methodology section.
- Recommendations for future research.

TABLE 6.3   Recommended lengths for different sections of the research report expressed as percentages of total word count

Abstract	2.5%
Literature review	30% (Introduction 5% of this)
Methodology	17.5%
Findings	30%
Discussion	20%

TABLE 6.4   Recommended lengths for different sections of a 6000-word research report expressed as number of words

Abstract	150
Literature review	1800
Methodology	1050
Findings	1800
Discussion	1200

Abstract – summary of complete text

The abstract is actually the first section of a research report, coming straight after the title. It can only be written after you have finished the whole report. The abstract is a challenge because it requires you to summarise the whole report in very few words. All four main sections of the report have to be covered in just a few sentences each.

Many students ask for guidance on how long the different sections should be. Tables 6.3 and 6.4 offer some suggestions. The percentages in Table 6.1 can be applied to reports of different sizes. Table 6.4 shows the word lengths for a 6000-word dissertation.

Remember, the figures are not exact, so you can have more or fewer words in each section, but they do give a general indication of the weighting of the different sections of a research report.

Student example: writing a dissertation

Sue was studying for a master's degree. The early part of the course required two essays. The first essay was a review of theory and research in her chosen area of undergraduate motivation for reading (including texts related to the undergraduates' course and non-course texts). The second essay focused on the methodological issues related to the research project that Sue was going to carry out. The final assessment was a dissertation. Once Sue had collected and analysed her data, she began drafting her dissertation. Her tutor advised her to write the findings chapter first because this was a new form of writing to her (she had some experience of literature review and methodology writing from her two essays). The tutor also advised that the final shape of the findings chapter would influence the writing of the dissertation more generally. For example, key themes that emerged from the findings would be used to focus the line of argument in the dissertation as a whole, and importantly would suggest things that could be deleted, not just the things that would be included.

Having submitted a second complete draft of her dissertation, Sue received feedback from her tutor that is shown in the first column of Table 6.5 (some further comments highlighting key points for the readers of this book are shown in the second column).

In general, the tutor concentrated on the larger structural features that need work first. Until these larger features are addressed, it is not productive to focus too much on the smaller but important elements such as precise use of language. Sue achieved a very good mark for her dissertation and passed her MPhil at a level that allowed her to proceed to PhD study.

DOS AND DON'TS

✓ Do

- think carefully about the overall structure of your writing
- use subheadings to title meaningful sections
- make sure that your paragraphs are complete, are the appropriate length and link together well

✗ Don't

- write one draft and think that the structure will be OK without revision and planning
- have paragraphs which are too long or too short
- repeat phrases and sentences by mistake

TABLE 6.5 Feedback on a dissertation

Feedback from tutor	Key general points for academic writing
You have done some very good work on the dissertation. There were many things I enjoyed reading, for example the explanation of the need for 'alternative paradigms'.	
In addition to much editing there are some bigger issues to attend to.	
Chapter 1 – Introduction	
p. 1 Do you present conclusive evidence for a decline in reading motivation? If not then don't assert that there has been a decline. See also the point about p. 7.	Be careful about asserting points without providing evidence or logical argument to support them.
p. 7 Para 2 is a vital aspect of your argument but quite rightly is covered in depth in the literature review. Perhaps you don't need to start this argument at all in the introductory section. At the moment it feels superficial.	Chapters in a dissertation are a mixture of in-depth analysis and summary sections that focus the line of argument and provide signposts to guide the reader.
Chapter 2 – Literature Review	
p. 2 Don't exaggerate the lack of research in the field. Simply show (not tell) what research there is, then in *one* place explain the need for your research.	Most students understand the importance of carrying out research that has not been done before but then repeat too often their claim to originality. The way to do this is to present a thorough account of relevant work in the field then summarise briefly how your work adds to this. At undergraduate level this is likely to be a very modest contribution. Remember there will be people in your field who have devoted their academic lives to your topic of interest so any claim you make about originality should be tentative.
p. 2 I suggest that you paraphrase Guthrie and Anderson so that you can put motivation before conceptual knowledge. This order fits your line of argument better.	Sequencing of chapters, sections, paragraphs, points is a persistent issue for all writers. Overall you must aim for a logical flow of points. However, this is made more complicated because other things have to be taken into account when structuring the writing, for example: the date that previous work that you are citing was published/ undertaken; the need to address big ideas (such as philosophical or societal ones) before more narrow technical ones; the chronology of tasks undertaken as part of the research versus the need for representing findings as concepts and categories.

(Continued)

TABLE 6.5 (Continued)

Feedback from tutor	Key general points for academic writing
p. 3 Para 2 is important to your argument but it is over-complicated at the moment. Make this clearer.	There is a need for clear writing about complicated ideas.
p. 4 Instead of 'this current study' it may be clearer to say 'my study'.	You are allowed to use 'I' or 'my' but it should be used sparingly in order to ensure the appropriate kind of language for formal academic writing.
Your general tone should be to talk about building and enriching the research field rather than being negatively critical.	There is a difference between criticism and critique. Criticism is negative whereas critique is constructive exploration of ideas and the presentation of an alternative perspective.
Research on undergraduates is your prime source for research studies. Consider always explaining these studies first before studies carried out with younger students in schools.	It is important to be selective about the studies that you cite – this is about rejecting studies that are less relevant. This is also an example of a sequencing issue (see above).
p. 7 You cite some interesting early studies but don't really describe what they found and how it is relevant to your study. Be more selective – choose the studies that are relevant rather than talk about the ones that are not relevant.	Some studies that you cite require more attention than others. For example, you need to decide how much information you need to give the reader about the methods used when citing research studies.
p. 9 Save your summary of why your study is different until after the review of literature including the review of socio-cultural work.	This is an example of a sequencing issue (see above).

Chapter 3 – Methodology

PAST TENSE throughout!	A common problem. Methodology chapters are often written before the research is carried out. The dissertation should in general be written in the past tense because it is a report of work that has been completed.
p. 4 Don't discuss interviewing methodology before the data collection section.	This was an example of a sequencing issue (see above).
p. 7 'Punjabi' is not an 'ethnicity'.	
p. 8 Is Seidman's three-interview series still relevant given that you only did two interviews? If it is you need to explain Seidman's ideas before saying how you modified them.	It is important to be very clear about the methods that you use. Find out how they were originally intended to be used then explain any modifications you make provided you have strong methodological reasons for doing so, and provided this does not render your use of the technique/ tool/approach invalid.

Feedback from tutor	Key general points for academic writing
One example of a transcript and one example of a reading experience log in the appendix would be good.	Students often ask how much raw data they should include in the dissertation. No more than 10% of raw data should be necessary, depending on the kind of research being carried out. It is often easier, and indeed necessary, to include a greater percentage of quantitative data.
Data analysis including the codes, their meanings and their hierarchies needs describing. Generally data analysis needs to be clearer.	Often a difficult section to write. Read research methods texts on data analysis, then carry out your analysis, then clearly explain in the dissertation how the analysis was carried out.

Chapter 4 – Findings

First para – do not summarise your findings here. Take us through the data first.	Although it is necessary to provide some indications to the reader of what to expect this can be overdone. Remember that the abstract to a dissertation is a summary. The introductory sections also tend to include an overview of what is to be covered in the dissertation. In relation to the findings chapter it is important to take the reader through your analyses before summarising the findings.
Keep the heading hierarchy to no more than three levels. Why numbered?	Numbering of subheadings tends to be a feature of very long reports. I am not in favour of numbering for dissertations because it can result in less attention to the natural flow of argument, but some institutions encourage numbering.
There appear to be rather a lot of direct quotes.	See Chapter 5 for guidance on quotations.
Shouldn't the three main themes that you describe at the end of the chapter be used as the basis for the organisation of the whole chapter?	For students writing-up qualitative research there is a close link between analysis and writing. Writing gives an opportunity to further evaluate the credibility of your analysis. It also enables you to focus more clearly on the main themes revealed by your data. In this case the student arrived at some very useful themes by the end of this draft of her findings chapter. In the end these themes became an important way to anchor the dissertation as a whole and ensure a coherent line of argument.

Chapter 5 – Discussion

Delete para 1.	Writers often write themselves into their writing. In other words the opening sentence/paragraph/page or even whole section may need to be deleted because the high quality writing emerges later.
Para 2 is important but not clear enough. How does this relate to the three main themes in the last chapter? Would a bullet point list of findings help in this chapter?	See the point above about themes.

(Continued)

TABLE 6.5 (Continued)

Feedback from tutor	Key general points for academic writing
6.3 [section in Sue's dissertation] is not really implications, it is more discussion. The implications are going to be brief and probably only two or three paras at most.	All the chapters in the dissertation have distinct information that needs to be presented. For example, methods and methodology should mainly be addressed in the methodology chapter and not in other chapters (apart from brief accounts of the methods used in selected studies in the literature review, or in the reflections on the limitations of the research that is normally included in the final chapter).

Minor issues

Please email in one file not separate chapter files

Use Higher Education (HE) instead of 'higher learning institute'?

p. 6 Grammar of UNESCO statement seems unusual

p. 8 Strange red text covering Vygotsky quote

socio-cultural not social cultural

Chapter 3 – NVivo not 'Envivo'

7

Grammar and Punctuation

The use of grammar is an essential part of the writing process. Having been shown the difference between prescriptive and descriptive grammar, you will see examples of many pitfalls. Common mistakes made by students are shown and the use of the grammar check on a word processor is examined. Punctuation marks are small in size yet very important in helping you to make your meaning clear. You will learn about the purpose of all the main punctuation marks. In order to help you think about your own use of punctuation, you will also read about the kinds of errors that students often make with punctuation marks.

Grammar

To start you thinking about grammar, here are a couple of puzzles to solve. Can you think of:

- a grammatical sentence with the word 'and' repeated five times in succession?
- a grammatical sentence with the word 'had' repeated nine times in succession?

You will find the answers at the end of the chapter.

Grammar is one of the most important parts of writing. It is the way that words and sentences are put together in order to express meaning. It is also one of those subjects, like apostrophes, neat handwriting, the Queen's English, and so on, that can make some people get quite worked up!

At the heart of many arguments about grammar are different views about how language works. Some people believe that there is a fixed set of grammatical rules which you simply have to learn in order to speak and write correctly. People with this view can be called *prescriptive grammarians* **G**.

Most modern linguists take a different view. They see language as something to be described and analysed in order to understand the way that it is used. *Descriptive grammarians* are interested in the way that all language use reflects a particular context, such as the social background of the speaker and the setting in which the message is communicated. This kind of information needs to be taken into account when analysing language and suggesting the rules that are at work. The idea that particular features of language are correct or incorrect is simply a product of someone's judgement, not an absolute rule. However, there can be no doubt that there are a wide range of language conventions that need to be followed if writing is to be seen to be 'correct'. And just in case you think I am suggesting that anything goes, the following sentence is definitely incorrect: rules are grammar no there for.

KEY FACT

Claims about incorrect language use typically focus on a tiny proportion of the language. In other words, more than 99 per cent of our speech does not cause anyone to claim that it is incorrect but there are a few phrases which repeatedly cause disagreement.

We also need to make a clear distinction between talking and writing. Talk is much less subject to standard conventions than writing and tends to be more informal, although occasions such as formal speeches are a different case. Writing is subject to more agreement about what is correct than talking, although the internet and other electronic texts continue to challenge this idea. Conventional or 'correct' writing is standardised by various authoritative sources such as major dictionaries, style guides (including publishers' in-house guides and those available more generally), books like this one, and computer packages/functions such as the grammar check. This greater standardisation of writing has occurred because there is the need for it to communicate without ambiguity to a wider range of people at ever greater distances.

★ TOP TIP

Think about grammar as a set of conventions to be learned rather than as fixed rules.

Improving your grammar requires you to learn to proofread each word, phrase, sentence and paragraph in your writing separately. You also have to read the words and phrases in the wider context of the sentence and para-graph and think carefully about whether they fit properly. In order to write conventional grammar in your assignments, you need to develop an 'ear' for academic language. In other words, you will learn when sentences 'sound' right. Improving your grammar can also be helped by recognising some of the common problems that students have and then applying this knowledge when looking carefully at your own writing.

Student example: test your grammar

A student was writing an essay about the National Literacy Strategy. Here's a quote from the essay. Cover the paragraph after next to see if you can work out the problems before you see the answers.

Various research evidence throughout the nineteen nineties looked at the teaching and learning of English and it was conclusive that pupils knowledge, skills and understand-ing in the area of English could be substantially increased. This was also evident in the results of the National Tests for English and therefore, the teaching of English education within schools needed improvement.

[1] Various research evidence throughout the [2] nineteen nineties looked at the teaching and learning of English and [3] it was conclusive that [4] pupils knowledge, skills and under-standing in the area of English could be substantially increased. This was also evident in the results of the [5] National Tests for English [6] and therefore, the teaching of English [7] education within schools needed improvement.

So many things to think about in only two sentences! The first thing to say about the student's writing extract above is that the two points are good ones:

1   In the 1990s it was felt that standards of pupils' reading and writing could be improved.
2   The statutory tests (or SATs in everyday language) indicated that standards could be better.

However, the good points are obscured by some of the grammatical problems. Let's have a look at each of the problems in turn:

1   Too wordy – the word "various" is not needed. 'Research evidence throughout the 1990s' would have been fine. To keep the word 'various' and be grammatically appropriate, the sentence would have to read 'Various pieces of research evidence' but then this sounds like there wasn't much research.
2   Unconventional – this is not incorrect but in a text like this it is conventional to put 1990s. Please note that there should not be an apostrophe after the zero (see Chapter 8).

3 Too wordy – 'and concluded that' or 'and it was concluded that' would be better.

4 Missing apostrophe – should be 'pupils' knowledge' because the student meant more than one pupil's knowledge.

5 Capital letters not needed – in general, capital letters are often overused in assignments. The name 'national curriculum' is an interesting case. When it was first used in 1988 it was normal to use capitals ('National Curriculum') but since then the convention has changed to no capitals unless it is part of the title in the reference list.

6 Slightly ambiguous – this is not incorrect but the point would be stronger if "and therefore" was replaced by the phrase 'adding further evidence that'. This has the effect of properly linking the second point about test results with the first point about research in the 1990s.

7 Too wordy – if "education within schools" is deleted then the point is clearer: the teaching of English needed improvement.

Grammar check on the word processor

The grammar check does raise your awareness of some of the common problems, and for that reason you should try using it. But like all computer packages, it has to work by using rigid rules. In fact, the grammar check is a perfect example of how prescriptive grammar is an inadequate way to think about language. The biggest problem for the computer is that it cannot understand your intended meaning and the particular context of the points that you are making. This can result in some dubious suggestions.

Anyway, it's all very well me telling you what to do but let's see how good my own grammar is. I carried out the grammar check on the first draft of this chapter (which was changed considerably to reach the final version that you see now).

- The text in bold is the issue that the grammar check identified for me.
- The text in italics is the example from the draft of this chapter.
- The final text in the box is the grammar check suggestion to help me correct my work.

Extra spaces

The grammar check spotted an extra space between two letters. It is an easy mistake to make and it is helpful to have it pointed out.

Capitalisation

*Language is always changing and 'sat watching' has become **s**tandard English.*

Suggestions: **S**tandard English.

Interesting – a perfect example of the way that language is constantly changing! *Chamber's Dictionary* says it should be 'standard English'. The *Oxford English Dictionary* (*OED*) says that it should be 'Standard English' but the examples of documents from 1836 to 1978 vary, with a trend towards using the capital letter in modern times.

Commonly confused words

Its *just wrong.*

Suggestions: It's.

Whoops – a bit of a typo there! The intended meaning was 'It is just wrong'. 'It's' is correct because it is a contraction of 'it is' (see Chapter 8).

'that' instead of 'which'

Unfortunately, this mistake can be a keyboard error or 'typo', **something which spell check** Ⓖ *will not pick up because the spelling is correct.*

Suggestions: 'something, which spell check', or 'something that spell check'.

The first suggestion ('something, which spell check') is nonsense and grammatically incorrect. The second suggestion makes no difference to the meaning. I won't be changing it but the publisher's proofreader might do!

Pronoun use

Which means that if someone tells you that you are wrong for using a split infinitive you can tell **them** *not to be such a prescriptive grammarian.*

Suggestions: him or her.

Publishers usually include guidance that tells us that we have to use words like 'them' in place of him/her to avoid gender-biased language, or, in other words, sexist stereotypes, so no change is needed.

Number agreement

*If I spend that amount of time on two **sentence** I'll never hit the deadlines.*

Suggestions: sentences.

Fair point, another typo there.

Compound words

*when you are **proof-reading***

Suggestions: proofreading.

I don't mind that – it's easier without the hyphen. Language tends to be simplified over time so things tend to be missed out rather than added – a process called 'redundancy' (unfortunately, the spell checker offers both the version with the hyphen and the one without, which contradicts the grammar check!).

So, overall, it looks as though the grammar check has been about 50 per cent correct. Personally, I don't find the grammar check very useful but you may find that it raises your awareness of some grammar issues. Make sure that you have the confidence to overrule it when it fails to understand your meaning properly.

More common grammar pitfalls

This chapter has already covered a number of common pitfalls:

1. misunderstanding the difference between prescriptive and descriptive grammar
2. writing which is too wordy
3. not understanding changing conventions like '1990s'
4. not understanding punctuation (for more on this subject, see Chapter 8)
5. not understanding when to use capital letters
6. ambiguous meaning
7. a lack of cohesion (the way that words, sentences and paragraphs link together to convey meaning)
8. poor spacing and layout

9   commonly confused words

10 grammatical agreement for the number of things you refer to in the sentence – this is usually about singular and plural

11 compound words like 'proofreading/proof-reading'.

To conclude the chapter, here are some other traps which many students fall into:

- Not understanding the subject that you are writing about – if you are struggling to understand some of the texts that you have to read to support your assignments this can result in poor grammar. If this is the case, go back to the texts, read them again, list the key points and make sure you understand before you redraft.

- Being too informal – we all use the way that we speak to help us write. After all, writing is just a way of representing spoken language. But writing has developed sophisticated conventions of its own which mean that it is different from speech and generally more formal.

> Here's an example of informal language: "a trimmer condensed version was introduced". There are two grammatical problems here. First, the word 'trimmer' is too informal. It is the sort of word you might use when talking to a friend but not when you are writing an essay. Second, the idea is repeated by the better phrase 'condensed version'. We call this kind of repetition 'tautology', which is basically saying the same thing twice. 'Trimmer' should have been deleted.

- Using mixed tenses – as a general rule, the tense should be the same throughout a piece of writing. Here's an example of a mixed tense resulting from a possible lack of understanding: "**In 2002** 80 per cent of 11-year-olds **are** expected". The student was writing in 2003 so the tense should have been 'were expected'. It is important to remember that the year of publication is not just a convention of the author/date citation: it means the year that the text was written. As in the example above, this can be significant for the point you are making.

- Which person? – Many people quite rightly point out that you should not use 'I' (first person) in an academic piece of writing (for example, 'I have found research showing that formal grammar teaching does not help writing'). Academic writing is often more effective when written in the third person ('**Researchers** have shown that formal grammar teaching does not help writing'). There are exceptions to this though. For example, you might be explaining what you personally did as part of teaching practice. It is perfectly OK to use 'I' occasionally but you do need to check how often and guard against overuse.

- Sentence length – If your sentences are too long, you are more likely to be unclear. On the other hand, too many short sentences can make the writing disjointed. Start the first draft of your writing with simple short sentences that are as clear as possible. Then work on making them flow. Sometimes you may join two short sentences together to improve the flow. Quite often, the choice of the first word in a sentence can make the difference between disjointed sentences and smoothly flowing ones.

Do not be downhearted if you find that you are making some grammatical mistakes. All writers make mistakes. I once applied for a job as a principal lecturer, a job which I got in spite of the fact that my letter of application was headed 'Principle Lecturer'. That is the kind of principle that you believe in, not the principal which means 'head of'. Not bad for the author of a book like this!

Punctuation

Punctuation marks are small in size yet very important in helping you to make your meaning clear. In this chapter, you will learn about the purpose of all the main punctuation marks. In order to help you think about your own use of punctuation, you will also read about the kinds of errors that students often make with punctuation marks.

The most basic punctuation mark is the full stop. We often say that a full stop is used to mark the end of a sentence but this begs the question 'what is a sentence?' People often say that a sentence is something that begins with a capital letter and ends with a full stop. This is a bit of a circular description if we are trying to explain a full stop: a full stop is used at the end of a sentence and a sentence has a full stop at the end! It is also linguistically inaccurate. Sentences sometimes end with question marks or exclamation marks. Many printed sentences lack punctuation, such as newspaper headlines. Spoken sentences do not have a capital letter and a full stop either. Having said that, it is very rare that we speak in the exact equivalent of written sentences; speech has different organisational and structural features.

Defining a sentence is not easy but the work of David Crystal (2004) is very helpful for this discussion. A sentence is:

- a construction which can be used on its own, without people feeling that it is incomplete
- the largest construction to which the rules of grammar apply (in a descriptive sense)
- constructed according to a system of rules which are naturally acquired by nearly all the mother-tongue speakers of the language. A sentence formed in this way is said to be grammatical (Crystal, 2004, p. 37).

Minor sentences such as 'Hello.' 'Eh?' 'Like father, like son.' 'Wish you were here.' 'Taxi!' are irregular. Major sentences are what we usually mean when we refer to sentences. There are two types of major sentence: a simple sentence and a multiple sentence.

A simple sentence contains one clause. A clause must contain a verb and is built from 'clause elements' (which consist of one or more words).

Clause element	Subject	Verb	Object
Clause (also a simple sentence in this example)	You	threw	a stone

KEY FACT

Clauses can have the following elements:

- subject (S)
- verb (V)
- object (O)
- complement (C) (further information about another clause element)
- adverbial (A) (further information about the situation).

There are seven basic clause types: S+V; S+V+O; S+V+C; S+V+A; S+V+O+O; S+V+O+C; S+V+O+A.

A multiple sentence contains more than one clause. There are two main types:

1   A *compound* sentence: the clauses, which could in principle stand as sentences on their own, are linked by coordinators such as 'and', 'or', 'but'. For example, *'I like his hat* [main clause] but *I don't like his coat.'* [main clause].

2   A complex sentence: the clauses are linked by subordination with words like 'because', 'when', 'although'. One clause (the subordinate clause) is subordinated to another (the main clause). The subordinate clause cannot stand as a sentence on its own because it relies grammatically on another clause. The information it contains is in the background compared to the main clause. For example, *'I answered the door* [main clause] *when Jane rang the bell.'* [subordinate clause]. (Crystal, 2004, p. 201)

All of that was a slightly lengthy explanation of why a sentence is not just something that begins with a capital letter and ends with a full stop! The simplest and most accurate description of a sentence is that it is something which makes complete sense on its own and *usually* begins with a capital letter and ends with a full stop.

The first step in using punctuation better is to know what the main punctuation marks are used for. Most of the explanations for these are more straightforward than the one for the full stop.

Understanding punctuation marks

Comma ,

A comma separates clauses and clause elements in a sentence in order to clarify meaning and to avoid ambiguity. If you read one of your sentences and it does not quite make sense, look at the use of commas and either delete or add a comma. Commas have many other uses but are used particularly to separate items in a list or items in sentences which have list-like structures. The comma indicates a slight pause in the flow of the sentence when reading aloud.

Semicolon ;

A semicolon separates main clauses that are not joined by a *coordinator* **G**, which the semicolon replaces. The two parts of the sentence feel equally important. A semicolon represents a break in the flow of the sentence which is stronger than a comma but weaker than a full stop. For example, The students in the first study were hard working; those in the second were lazy.

 KEY FACT

A *coordinator* is a word which links parts of a sentence. The most common coordinators are 'and', 'or' and 'but'. Some people call these conjunctions.

Colon :

A colon separates a first clause, which could stand as a sentence, from a final phrase or clause that extends or illustrates the first clause. It is most commonly used to introduce things, like lists or an example. See paragraph two of this punctuation section (p.101) for an example of the use of a colon mid-sentence.

★ **TOP TIP**

If in doubt about using a colon or semicolon mid-sentence, try rewording the sentence or using a comma instead.

Apostrophe '

This is the punctuation mark that probably catches more students out than any other. There are four main uses:

- contraction: didn't = did not
- possession singular: the cat's tail, the child's book
- possession plural: the cats' tails, the children's books (as 'children' is an irregular plural word, the apostrophe comes before the 's')
- possession with name ending in 's': Donald Graves's book (although Donald Graves' book is not incorrect).

Common errors include:

1 'This first happened in the 60's' – logically, '60s' is plural, not a contraction. However, in the past '60's' was used as a way to signal plural but the convention has changed to '60s' in recent times.
2 'Was that it's name?' – confusion between 'its' (possessive) and 'it's' (contraction of 'it is'). This possessive form is irregular and does *not* have an apostrophe as in 'Was that its name?'

Parenthesis (including brackets)

This can be indicated with dashes (–) or commas but is most effective with brackets (such as the ones surrounding this comment).

Parenthesis means structurally independent words or phrases which elaborate the meaning of sentences and which are often separated by brackets ( ). Square brackets [ ] are used in academic writing to indicate that the words have been added by you and should not be confused with the quoted source.

> The Literacy and Numeracy Strategies have, according to all those who have evaluated them, been strikingly successful at improving the quality of teaching and raising standards in primary schools. *But we need to embed the lessons of the National Literacy and Numeracy Strategies more deeply* [italics added]. (Department for Education and Skills, 2003, p. 27)

Hyphen -

A hyphen links words or phrases to clarify meaning; and indicates that words are part of a single expression. For example:

- We must re-form the group.
- The children were involved in role-play.

Dash –

The length of the line is given different names. One name is the *en-dash* (–), which is used to indicate a page range, e.g. pp. 23–35, or mark parenthesis. The *em-dash* (—) is longer and can also be used to mark parenthesis. It can further be used to indicate part of a sentence added as an afterthought but I would recommend that a comma is often better for this. In reality, we usually use the hyphen key on the keyboard for most of these uses because it is easier than using the insert menu's *insert symbol, special characters* function. *Autocorrect* normally inserts the appropriate dash but you may need to check this.

Slash /

A slash is often used to indicate words or phrases that are used interchangeably. For example, the statutory tests/SATs were carried out on the same day.

Ellipsis ...

Shown by three dots, an ellipsis indicates where something has been omitted. It is often used to show that part of the text from a quote has been omitted. It is also used in fiction writing to indicate an unfinished thought or to imply continuation of thinking.

Quotation marks " " or ' '

Systems for using single or double quotation marks vary, but whichever system you use it's important to be consistent. The advice I offer here follows the style of some top journals.

Double quotation marks are used to enclose a quote from a published source of less than 40 words (use single marks within the double quotation marks for material that was enclosed in double marks in the original source, i.e. to indicate a quote within a quote).

Long quotations of more than 40 words (see Chapter 5) are spaced and indented, and are not enclosed within quotation marks (use double quote marks to enclose material that was in quotation marks within the original). If punctuation is part of the quoted material then place it within the quotation marks.

Single quotation marks are used to show that an expression is in everyday use but that it is not academically precise. They can also be used to indicate that you are referring to the word or letter in question rather than using it as a normal part of the sentence. Single marks are often used to enclose direct speech in works of fiction. Single quotation marks enclose the title of a journal article or the chapter of a book if mentioned in the main text.

Italics are used to indicate the title of a book, journal, magazine or film. They are also used for the introduction of a new, technical or key term or label the first time it is used but not subsequently.

Student examples: problems with punctuation

Let's look at some of the ways that students typically misuse punctuation marks.

Full stop

> The girl was relying mostly on the story and her knowledge of language to help her decode words. Which is good because it means that she is using sensible strategies and understands what she is reading but the phonic errors suggest this is an area which could be improved.

The problem is with the full stop in the section "help her decode words. Which is …". Normally you would expect the sentence to continue without any punctuation at this point. The student realised that if this was the case the sentence would be very long and so tried to break it up with punctuation. This was a good idea but it required changes to the grammar to match the change to the punctuation. My suggestion would be:

> The girl was using her knowledge of the story and her knowledge of language to help the decoding of words. These were effective strategies which particularly helped her understanding of the meaning of the story, but phonic miscues suggested that her phonological understanding was an area for improvement.

The use of tense always requires careful handling; notice how I changed the example to past tense. The interesting thing here is the way that I have had to make a number of changes to the meaning in order to correct what appears to be a routine problem with a full stop. My own knowledge of the subject of the writing is an important part of this. Quite often, a lack of full understanding of the concepts and issues that the student is grappling with shows itself in weak grammar and punctuation. These changes show that, as with all things in the writing process, it is not simply a case of obeying a rule.

★ TOP TIP

If your punctuation seems to be wrong, it may be because your understanding of the topic you are writing about is not strong enough. Go back to your planning and think again about the points that you are making. If necessary, do some more reading and thinking, and then redraft your writing.

Comma

> Over the last forty years psychologists discovered children know a lot implicitly about how language works, and they use this knowledge to form expectations about meaning from speech, along with written language as long as it is in a meaningful context.

The first comma is unnecessary because the meaning is clear without it. The second comma is also unnecessary for the same reason and because it provides an unnecessary break in the flow of the sentence. However, if you take the commas out the sentence does not communicate its meaning clearly, mainly because it is too long. The following is better:

> Over the last forty years psychologists have discovered much more about children's implicit knowledge. Children's language knowledge results in them having an expectation that speech and writing communicate

meaning. In order to derive meaning from written language young children in particular benefit from writing being part of a meaningful context.

Once again, the problem is not simply one of re-punctuating. In particular, the point made in the final sentence is not sufficiently developed. It would probably need a new paragraph with some examples and further explanation offered.

Quotation marks

The 'look and say' approach teaches children to recognise whole words rather than looking at the individual letters.

The quotation marks should be single because this is an expression, not a quotation.

Colon (and a few other things)

Try and work out the mistakes in the following paragraph before you look at the answers. Once you have understood the points repeat the exercise, without looking at the answers, in order to help your memory of things to look for.

Smith (Smith, 1994) gave a few simple rules to the volunteers, "If the mistake doesn't make sense, then prompt with a clue about the meaning of the story. If the mistake makes sense, prompt with a clue about the way the word looks. If the reader does not say anything ask them to read to the end of the sentence or go back to the beginning of the sentence again."

Smith[1] ([2]Smith,[3] 1994) gave a few simple rules to the volunteers,[4] "[5]If the mistake doesn't make sense,[6] then prompt with a clue about the meaning of the story. If the mistake makes sense, prompt with a clue about the way the word looks. If the reader does not say anything ask them to read to the end of the sentence or go back to the beginning of the sentence again."[7]

Here are the explanations for the mistakes:

1 Don't repeat the name for a citation.
2 In this context, the bracket should be before the year, not before the name.
3 The comma is not necessary if the bracket is moved and the repeat of the name deleted.
4 This should be a colon, not a comma, because the student is introducing a quote which extends the first part of the sentence.
5 The quotation should be moved to a new line and indented because it is more than 39 words long, which means that quotation marks are not needed. They would be if the quote was less than 40 words.

6   The comma is not necessary but should be kept if the original source included it.

7   The page number of the quotation is needed. The quotation mark is not needed if the quote is set out appropriately.

Here's how the paragraph should have been punctuated:

Smith (1994) gave a few simple rules to the volunteers:

> If the mistake doesn't make sense then prompt with a clue about the meaning of the story. If the mistake makes sense prompt with a clue about the way the word looks. If the reader does not say anything ask them to read to the end of the sentence or go back to the beginning of the sentence again. (Smith, 1994, p. 23)

DOS AND DON'TS

✓ **Do**

- understand that grammar is about conventions, not fixed rules
- appreciate the links between meaning, grammar and punctuation
- learn to recognise your common mistakes by comparing them with some of the ones in this chapter

✗ **Don't**

- make your language unnecessarily complicated
- use language which is too informal
- forget that every word counts

Answers to puzzles

1   A fish and chip shop owner is replacing his shop sign but the sign writer writes 'fishand-chips'. The owner says, 'You should leave a gap between "fish" and "and" and "and" and "chips"'.

2   During a discussion with two students about an assignment that they had just done, the tutor raised the issue of whether a key point should have been: (i) 'Andrew had a lot of problems' or (ii) 'Andrew had had a lot of problems'. Jill had used 'had' and Jack had changed his from 'had had' to 'had'. The tutor observed that, 'Jack, where Jill had had "had", had had "had had"; "had had" was correct'.

Not the most elegant grammar I admit! If you are struggling to understand the meaning of the sentence, the logic is as follows:

- Jack had originally used the phrase 'had had'.
- At the same point in the assignment, Jill had used the phrase 'had'.
- 'Had had' was the correct phrase.

8

Spelling

The history of the development of English has resulted in its spelling being difficult to learn. One of the first things that you need to think about is your problem words. You are shown how to think actively about these in order to remember them. You are also given other ideas about how to remember words.

Why is English spelling so tricky? It is mainly because it is not a phonologically regular language like Spanish or Finnish. George Bernard Shaw cleverly illustrated this. Do you know what 'ghoti' means? The answer is 'fish'. If you take the sound of 'gh' in enough, the 'o' in women, and the 'ti' in station you get fish! It is the irregularities of English spelling that make it demanding to learn.

One of the main reasons that English spelling is phonetically irregular is because of the many ways through history that it has been influenced. It was during the fifth century that the Anglo-Saxons settled in England and, as always happens when people settle, they bring changes to the language, a process that resulted in 'Old English' being established. The texts that have survived from the period are in four main dialects: West Saxon, Kentish, Mercian and Northumbrian. The last two are sometimes grouped together and called Anglian. West Saxon became the standard dialect at the time but is not the direct ancestor of modern standard English, which is mainly derived from an Anglian dialect (Barber, 1993). If we take the modern word 'cold' as an example, the Anglian 'cald' is the stronger influence as opposed to the West Saxon version, 'ceald'.

In the ninth century, the Vikings brought further changes to the language. Place names were affected: 'Grimsby' meant Grim's village and 'Micklethwaite' meant large clearing. The pronunciation of English speech was affected at this time and it is possible to recognise some Scandinavian influenced words because of their phonological form. It is suggested that 'awe' is a Scandinavian word and that this came from changes of pronunciation in the Old English word 'ege'. One of the most interesting things about Scandinavian *loanwords* ⓖ is that they are so commonly used: sister, leg, neck, bag, cake, dirt, fellow, fog, knife, skill, skin, sky, window, flat, loose, call, drag, and even 'they' and 'them' (Barber, 1993).

In more recent times, words from a range of countries have been borrowed. Here is a small selection of examples:

French – elite, liaison, menu, plateau
Spanish and Portuguese – alligator, chocolate, cannibal, embargo, potato
Italian – concerto, balcony, casino, cartoon
Indian – bangle, cot, juggernaut, loot, pyjamas, shampoo
African languages – banjo, zombie, rumba, tote.

However, for many of these words it is difficult to attribute them to one original country. To illustrate the complexities of detecting where words originated, consider the word 'chess':

'Chess' was borrowed from Middle French in the fourteenth century. The French word was, in turn, borrowed from Arabic, which had earlier borrowed it from Persian 'shah' ('king'). Thus the etymology of the word reaches from Persian, through Arabic and Middle French, but its ultimate source (as far back as we can trace its history) is Persian.

Similarly, the etymon of 'chess', that is, the word from which it has been derived, is immediately 'esches' and ultimately 'shah'. Loanwords have, as it were, a life of their own that cuts across the boundaries between languages. (Pyles and Algeo, 1993, p. 286)

The influence of loanwords is one of the factors that has resulted in some of the irregularities of English spelling. David Crystal (1997) lists some of the other major factors. Above, we referred to the Anglo-Saxon period; at this time there were only 24 graphemes (letter symbols) to represent 40 phonemes (sounds). Later 'i' and 'j', 'u' and 'v' were changed from being interchangeable to having distinct functions and 'w' was added but many sounds still had to be signalled by combinations of letters.

After the Norman Conquest, French scribes – who had responsibility for publishing texts – re-spelled a great deal of the language. They introduced new conventions such as 'qu' for 'cw' (queen), 'gh' for 'h' (night), and 'c' before 'e' or 'i' in words such as 'circle' and 'cell'. Once printing became better established in the West, this added further complications. William Caxton (1422–1491) is often credited with the 'invention' of the printing press but this is not accurate. During the seventh century, the Chinese printed the earliest known book *The Diamond Sutra,* using inked, wooden relief blocks. By the beginning of the fifteenth century, the process had developed in Korea to the extent that printers were manufacturing bronze type sets of 100,000 pieces. In the West, Johannes Gutenberg (1390s–1468) is credited with the development of a moveable metal type in association with a hand-operated printing press.

Many of the early printers working in England were foreign (especially from Holland) and used their own spelling conventions. Also, until the sixteenth century, line justification (lining up the beginnings and ends of lines) was achieved by changing words rather than by adding spaces. Once printing became established, the written language did not keep pace with the considerable changes in the way words were spoken, resulting in weaker links between sound and symbol.

The publication of Samuel Johnson's dictionary in 1755 was a very important moment in relation to English spelling. Noah Webster, the first person to write a major account of American English (and someone whose name is still celebrated in the most important American dictionary: *Webster's Third New International Dictionary*), compared Johnson's contribution to Isaac Newton's in mathematics. Johnson's dictionary was significant for a number of reasons. Unlike dictionaries of the past that tended to concentrate on 'hard words', Johnson wanted a scholarly record of the whole language. It was based on words in use and introduced a literary dimension, drawing heavily on writers such as Dryden, Milton, Addison, Bacon, Pope and Shakespeare (Crystal, 1997, p. 109). Shakespeare's remarkable influence on the English language is not confined to the artistic significance of his work – many of the words and phrases of his plays are still commonly used today:

> He coined some 2,000 words – an astonishing number – and gave us countless phrases. As a phrasemaker there has never been anyone to match him. Among his inventions: one fell swoop, in my mind's eye, more in sorrow than in anger, to be in a pickle, bag and baggage, vanish into thin air, budge an inch, play fast and loose, go down the primrose path, the milk of human kindness, remembrance of things past, the sound and fury, to thine own self be true, to be or not to be, cold comfort, to beggar all description, salad days, flesh and blood, foul play, tower of strength, to be cruel to be kind, and on and on and on and on. And on. He was so wildly prolific that he could put two in one sentence, as in Hamlet's observation: "Though I am native here and to the manner born, it is a custom more honoured in the breach than the observance." He could even mix metaphors and get away with it, as when he wrote: "Or to take arms against a sea of troubles." (Bryson, 1990, p. 57)

Johnson's work resulted in dictionaries becoming used as the basis for 'correct' usage for the first time. Dictionaries have a major role in the standardisation of language and it is interesting to note that standard American English is represented by *Webster's* dictionary but standard (English) English is represented by the *Oxford English Dictionary* (although *Chambers* dictionary is the main source for word games and crosswords).

David Crystal (2004) makes the point that although spelling is an area where there is more agreement about what is correct than other areas, there is still considerable variation. Sidney Greenbaum's (1986) research looked at all the words in a medium-sized desk dictionary beginning with A that were spelled in more than one way; he found 296. When extrapolating this to the dictionary as a whole, he estimated 5000 variants altogether, which is 5.6 per cent. If this were to be done with a dictionary as complete as the *Oxford English Dictionary*, this would mean many thousands of words where the spelling has not been definitively agreed. Crystal gives some of the examples including: accessory/accessary; acclimatize/acclimatise; adrenalin/adrenaline; aga/agha; ageing/aging; all right/alright. Many of Greenbaum's words were pairs but there were some triplets, for example, aerie/aery/eyrie and even quadruplets: anaesthetize/anaesthetise/anesthetize/anesthetise. Names translated from a foreign language compound the problems: Tschaikovsky/Chaikovsky/Tschaikofsky/Tchaikofsky/Tshaikovski; this is particularly so for music students.

The publishing process also has a significant influence on standardisation of the language. For example, most publishers have in-house style guides for authors and editors. If you take citing and referencing as an example, there are a number of different accepted ways of doing this, with the *Publication Manual of the American Psychological Association* being a significant example of a style guide (see Chapter 5). There are also independently published guides such as *Fowler's Modern English Usage* (which isn't quite as modern as it suggests) and guides like this one which contribute to the attempts to standardise the language.

Examples of spelling problems

An influence on standardisation of language that has not been emphasised in linguistics texts is computer software packages such as the word processor. The computer spell checker works by combining words from its dictionary with words that are in your personal dictionary. It has already had a positive impact on helping to reduce the number of spelling errors in students' writing. I am of course presupposing (and recommending) that you will use a word processor for your writing, although there are still some students who do their writing by hand, which means that they cannot benefit from the computer spell checker. Some professional writers also prefer to write by hand but they have the benefit that their work will be read by copyeditors and proofreaders whose job is to spot the errors and root them out. Unfortunately, you do not have the luxury of a professional proofreader to help you with your writing – it would be nice though, wouldn't it? The idea that writers work with other people to get feedback on their work is an important one. Although good writing is always driven by the main author, writers nearly always rely on other people as part of the complete process. So it is a good idea to work with your peers to support your writing (while ensuring that it is your own work) and in particular proofreading, including spelling.

The majority of spelling problems in education students' writing are more to do with grammar than a lack of understanding about how to spell particular words. Let's have a look at some examples.

> **Incorrect**: "will give the teacher ideas about were a child is in their learning"
>
> **Correct**: 'will give the teacher ideas about where a child is in their learning'

Sometimes this mistake is a typo and in some parts of the country it relates to the way that 'were' is pronounced. Apart from the spelling/grammar problem, the language of the extract is not precise enough. A better wording might have been 'will give the teacher ideas to assess the child's learning'; this avoids the original problem altogether.

> **Incorrect**: "investigating what areas where like in the past"
>
> **Correct**: 'investigating what areas were like in the past'

This is the same error reversed.

Just in case you think that this is a rather basic mistake, here is a quote from the first page of the May 2005 edition of the British Educational Research Association (BERA) journal *Research Intelligence*:

> One of the challenges of the BERA conference is that different groups want very different things from it. Traditionally it has been seen primarily as a conference for the educational research community itself; a place were researchers, whether just starting out or well established, can talk to colleagues in a supportive and open atmosphere.

> **Incorrect**: "which meant she rusted the activities"
>
> **Correct**: 'which meant she rushed the activities'

Definite typing error here. The 'T' is close to the 'H' on the keyboard. Unfortunately, 'rusted' is spelled correctly, so is not picked up by the spell checker, but obviously does not make sense in the context.

Incorrect: "comparing the seaside now to what it use to be like in the past"

Correct: 'comparing the seaside now to what it used to be like in the past'

Sometimes in the course of changing the tense of a piece of writing you can miss some of the other words that need changing.

Incorrect: "which is an on going type of assessment"

Correct: 'which is an ongoing type of assessment'

This is really a hyphen problem but, once again, the spell check does not pick this up, although the grammar check might do.

The problems with homophones

People who learn to write beyond GCSE level are able to accurately spell most of the words that they need to use. But we all have a number of words that we persistently misspell. Here are some of the words that over time I personally have wrestled with.

Effect and affect

The way I sorted these out was through grammatical understanding. I mainly use 'effect' as a noun; to remind myself I think about 'special effects'. I mainly use 'affect' as a verb which might be used in 'the activity affected the pupil's motivation'. However, when you look them up in the dictionary you see that they can be used in a wide range of ways and confusingly both can be either a noun or a verb.

Practice and practise

These two are important for education students who have to think about teaching practice and practising their teaching skills. As you saw in the last sentence, I mainly use 'practice' as a noun whereas I use 'practise' mostly as a verb.

Principle and principal

We need to go back to first principles on this one! 'Principal' can be remembered by the idea that an American head teacher is called a principal, whereas 'principle' is something that forms the basis for thought and/or action.

Inquiry and enquiry

A public inquiry is something that frequently is reported in the media. The *Oxford English Dictionary* says that 'enquire' is an alternative form of 'inquire'. Other dictionaries say that 'inquire' is standard English but 'enquire' is still very frequently used, especially in the sense 'to ask a question'.

Let's and lets

Use 'let's', a contraction, when you mean 'let us'. Use 'lets', a verb, when you mean 'allows' or 'rents'.

Who's and whose

Use 'who's', a contraction, when you mean 'who is'. Use 'whose', a pronoun, to indicate possession – for example, 'Whose books are these?'

How to improve your spelling

Each time we use the computer spell checker (or proofread our writing), we are given a reminder about the words we spell wrongly. In order to learn how to remember these words we need to think more actively. First of all, you need to identify which letter(s) in the word you find difficult to remember. Next, try and think of a logical way of breaking the word into smaller parts. It can be helpful to think about stems, *prefixes* Ⓖ and *suffixes* Ⓖ. Finally, try and use analogies with other similar words to help you remember the word next time. The key aspect of the similar words is that they share visual characteristics more than aural characteristics. In other words, they look similar rather than sound similar.

 KEY FACT

A prefix consists of a letter or letters placed at the front of a word or stem to form a new word: for example, in 'before'/'be-fore', 'be' is the prefix and 'fore' is the stem. A suffix consists of a letter or letters placed at the end of a word or stem to form a new word: for example, in 'shorten'/'short-en', 'short' is the stem and 'en' is the suffix.

You also need to develop a range of other strategies to help you remember problem words. Here are some suggestions:

1   Think about spelling 'rules'. Although there are always exceptions to spelling rules, the process of thinking about them and investigating the extent to which they work can help to improve spelling. One of the best-known rules is: *i* before *e* except after *c* when the sound is /ee/: for example, 'field' or 'receive'.

2   Another rule is that for words ending with a single consonant, preceded by a short vowel sound, you should double the consonant before adding the suffix: for example, split – splitting; bet – betted.

3   Develop the visual memory. Margaret Peters argued that spelling is largely a visual memory skill so she encouraged teachers to use the strategy of 'look, cover, write, check'. This involves looking at the correct spelling of a problem word, covering it, attempting to write it and then checking to see if you wrote it correctly (Peters, 1985).

4   Consider mnemonics and other devices. Think of 'necessary' as two ships on the sea, or two sleeves and one collar (two *ss* and one *c*).

5   Sound out words as they look. An example of this is: /bus/ /ee/ /ness/ for business.

6   Use a dictionary. A good dictionary, such as *Chambers* or *Longmans*, is a fascinating resource. Look up your problem words and read about their different meanings, and the different grammatical functions that they have. Greater knowledge about words and seeing them in the context of the dictionary can help jog your memory when you next come to write them.

7   Play word games. Games like *Scrabble, Boggle, Double Quick, and Lexicon*; crosswords; word searches and so on all require standard spelling. One of the interesting aspects of Scrabble is the way that very good players know all the more than 100 two-letter words that there are. As part of your knowledge of word structures, it can be interesting to look at the way that two- and three-letter words are built on to construct other words.

DOS AND DON'TS

✓ Do

- try the range of ways to improve your spelling suggested in this chapter
- use a spell checker
- think about how you can remember spellings

✗ Don't

- underestimate the importance of spelling
- ignore the words that you have difficulty with
- forget that English spelling has many visual letter patterns which can help you learn words

9

Presentation and Proofreading

You can greatly improve your writing by learning to proofread better. Having read this chapter you will understand the importance of keyboard skills and handwriting skills for exams. You will also learn some key messages about PowerPoint. The chapter concludes with a proofreading test based on a student's work.

One of the traps that many students fall into is to think that the more special effects there are in a text the more exciting it is. Shakespeare's comment that 'all that glistens is not gold' is relevant here. The best kind of academic presentation is one that least obscures the points that you are putting forward. To put this another way, the presentation should simply enhance what you are saying by not being obtrusive. You should not feel that a piece of writing that follows all the conventions accurately is a boring one. On the contrary, if your message is well researched and the language you use is effective this can be very exciting for the reader, particularly if they learn something themselves.

The internet has good examples of the principle of the presentation not interfering with access to the message. The best internet sites are those which are logically laid out and allow you to access their information quickly. They tend not to have dramatic presentation effects. Good examples of this style include the Amazon internet bookstore or the Kelkoo price comparison site. Berger and Wyse's site is much more artistic than these other examples but still has a simple logical structure combined with imaginative artwork, sound and visual effects.

I have argued throughout the book that I think that you should be using the computer for as much of your work as possible. This means that you will be using a keyboard rather than pen or pencil. Unfortunately, most people rely on two-finger typing for something which occupies them for large amounts of their time. I would urge you to get hold of a typing-tutor package and teach yourself to type properly. When I started my teaching career I was increasingly using the computer to prepare school documents. I decided to try a typing-tutor package. At first, it was quite slow-going and pretty boring, but I persevered. By the time I finished the package, I knew which fingers should be used for the different keys but I could not touch-type. From that point onwards, I made myself use the appropriate keys when working on a document. Gradually, through familiarisation, I began to memorise the positions of the keys and the most appropriate fingers to use. I can now touch-type which means that my speed of work has been greatly increased.

★ TOP TIP

Teach yourself to type with a computer software package.

Handwriting

The time when you typically cannot use a computer is during written exams. This is when handwriting is a particularly important skill. If an examiner comes across a script that is very poorly written, it does not put them in a good frame of mind. Primarily this is because they are under pressure to ensure that all scripts are marked to a deadline. A poorly written script means that they will have to take much longer to read it. Although this should not affect your mark if the points that you make are appropriate, poor presentation like this does have a subconscious negative impact on the marker. I even once heard an apocryphal story of an examiner who was under so much pressure that they decided to award an overall mark to each of the scripts based on handwriting alone! So, if your handwriting is poor, you should do something about it.

The goal of improving your handwriting should be towards a legible, fluent and comfortable style. Learning to form the individual letters of the alphabet and produce legible handwriting at a reasonable speed involves complex perceptuo-motor skills. Sassoon (2003) puts forward the concepts behind our writing system. Direction, movement and height are all crucial: left to right and top to bottom; the fact that letters have prescribed flowing movements with specific starting and exit points; and the necessity to ensure that letters have particular height differences. In addition, the variance between upper and lower case must be recognised and correct spacing consistently applied. Sassoon suggests that speed – but not too much speed – is also important as this can lead to fluency and greater efficiency. In exams it is necessary to think and write reasonably quickly.

Sassoon also advocates different levels of handwriting at different times. A calligraphic standard for special occasions might require a careful, deliberate approach, which will be more time-consuming than a legible, day-to-day hand. There are also times when you are drafting text or making notes, which you alone will read, where a lower standard of legibility will be appropriate.

In order to focus your attention on some of the key features of handwriting, it is helpful to define some terms. *Ascenders* are the vertical lines that rise above the midline (or x-line) on letters like 'd'; *descenders* are the vertical lines that hang below the baseline on letters like 'g'. Most letters have an 'entry stroke' where you start the letter and an *exit stroke*. Some letters like 'i' may not have entry or exit strokes and are called *sans serif*, meaning without the stroke (the origin of 'serif' is obscure but possibly came from a Dutch word). The letter 't' is interesting in that its horizontal line is called a *crossbar* and the height of the letter should only be three-quarters. This means that the top of the letter finishes between the midline and the ascender line. You will have worked out that there are four important horizontal lines: the *descender line*, the *baseline*, the *mid-line* and the *ascender line*. For adults only the baseline is visible; for children other lines have to be used carefully because there is a danger that they can measure the length of a stroke by the distance to the line and not by understanding the differences in letter size.

Sassoon (2003) recommends learning the handwriting joins in the following families of letters:

- letters which join easily from the baseline: acdehiklmntu
- letters which join easily from the top or the crossbar: orvw ft
- letters which can be joined with loops if you wish: yjgf
- other letters where joins are optional: bpqu
- letters that are better not joined: zxs
- letters joined with a movement which goes over the top and back except for e: ia ic id ig io iq ie
- capital letters can also be grouped in families although they do not join:
  - straight lines: ILT FEH
  - line and arch: UJ
  - circular: CUQGD PRB
  - diagonal: NMVWYAKX
  - counterchange: SZ.

Posture and working space are important elements of handwriting. For right-handed people, the paper is tilted to about 45 degrees anti-clockwise. It is important that the writing implement is not gripped too hard as this can lead to muscle tension in the shoulder and pain in the wrist and hand. Left-handed handwriting requires the paper to be turned clockwise to about 45 degrees and avoidance of holding the pen or pencil too near to the point.

Presentations

In addition to written assignments and exams, many students are encouraged to give presentations, which may or may not be assessed. The main function of a presentation is oral communication about a topic. It is important to remember the word 'oral' in this context. The worst kinds of presentations that I have seen are those which feature the presenter simply reading aloud a script. Students who come for interview are penalised if they do this in their presentations, just as you would be penalised in an assessed presentation. However nerve-wracking it is, you must develop the confidence to move away from reading aloud from a script. The few examples where this is necessary include television presenters, who have to do this because of the challenges of live television. The autocue reminds them of the words that they have to say. High-level politicians frequently have to rely on scripts (often written by other people) because it is difficult for them to improvise on the many subjects that they have ultimate responsibility for.

Presentation software such as *PowerPoint* has become very popular. PowerPoint can be used effectively as an aide-memoire when you are giving a presentation. At its most basic you can think of PowerPoint as simply an electronic version of the overhead transparency (OHT) and overhead projector (OHP). One of the main benefits of PowerPoint is the ability to show pictures of things like children's drawing and writing, which you would have to photocopy for the audience at considerable expense. PowerPoint also allows the audience to have a visual reminder of what you are saying. But there are many things that you should be careful about when using PowerPoint.

The basic principle that I outlined at the beginning of this chapter, that presentation should enhance (and not obscure) the points that you are making, is just as true for PowerPoint as it is for a written assignment. One of the important things about any text is its overall structure (see Chapter 6); PowerPoint is just another form of text. You need to understand the structure of a presentation as a whole. The *outline view* in PowerPoint allows you to build the presentation in a very similar way to the plan for an assignment. This gives you a much clearer view of the structure than trying to build the presentation slide by slide in 'slide' view. You should take care of the hierarchies of headings which reflect the logic of your message. If you ensure that you have a logical structure which supports the things that you are trying to communicate, your presentation will be better than one in which the audience are struggling to see how things relate.

The use of images which form an integral and necessary part of your presentation is good. The use of *Clip Art* just for the sake of improving the look is not good, because the audience may be thinking, what is the relevance of these images to the message? If sounds and music are directly relevant to your presentation then use them but the use of sound effects between slides does not really add much to your message. It is nearly always better to avoid the pre-prepared styles and use your own designs instead, because this is more likely to enhance your message.

Edward Tufte (2003) provides some very useful cautions about PowerPoint. Compared to text on paper, PowerPoint has very low resolution. So if you are presenting information with a lot of numbers, such as statistical information, it is a good idea to photocopy tables for the audience. The quality, relevance and integrity of the content of your presentations are what you will ultimately be judged on, not how pretty they look. Impressive-looking slides do not mask weak content. Tufte even showed that the choice of a PowerPoint presentation rather than a longer narrative structure was a factor in the death of the astronauts in the Columbia shuttle disaster.

> The choice of headings, arrangement of information, and size of bullets on the key chart served to highlight what management already believed. The uncertainties and assumptions that signalled danger dropped out of the information chain when the Mission Evaluation Room manager condensed the Debris Assessment Team's formal presentation to an informal verbal brief at the Mission Management Team meeting ... as information gets passed up an organization hierarchy, from people who do analysis to mid-level managers to high-level leadership, key explanations and supporting information is filtered out. In this context, it is easy to understand how a senior manager might read this PowerPoint slide and not realize that it addresses a life-threatening situation. (Tufte, 2003, p. 10)

In other words, unnecessarily complicated hierarchies which were part of the presentation, and the poor use of PowerPoint resulted in vital information being lost, leading to a lack of necessary action in relation to the disaster.

Proofreading

Proofreading is a demanding skill for all writers but it is one that gets better with thought and practice. Although my proofreading continues to improve, I am still not as efficient as a professional proofreader. If you are tackling new forms of writing, proofreading is even harder than it is for forms that you are more familiar with. First and foremost it requires you to have the attitude that mistakes really do matter. If your attitude is that you don't really care, you will need to change it, if you want to improve. You will also need to start taking an active interest in the way that language works and its conventions. The fact that you have bought this book is already a really good step along the road to becoming a better writer! Overall you need to develop your ear for language and learn to read like a writer.

Learn to see writing as a series of drafts. When you are doing the first drafts, you need to concentrate on getting the words down. Don't worry about errors at this point, just keep writing. There is no point trying to correct errors at the level of the sentence if the overall structure of the text has not been settled (go back to Chapter 3 and read the section on retrospective planning as a way of checking whether the overall structure is ready). Once you are happy with the overall structure, it is time to get down to the nitty-gritty. Or is it? One of the difficulties for any writer is detaching themselves from the message of their writing. If you try and move straight from composing to proofreading, you may find it difficult because you keep attending to the message rather than the surface features of the language. If time allows, you should leave the writing for a while; the longer the better so that you can return to it with fresh eyes. Imagine yourself wearing at least two different hats. The first hat is your 'author' hat. When you have got this hat on, you should work on the message until the writing says what you want it to say. Your second hat is the 'proofreader' hat. When you have got this hat on, you must look carefully at every word and sentence to correct the grammar, spelling, punctuation and presentation.

As the deadline approaches, it is then time to really get down to the proofreading. Try starting with the sentences in the first paragraph. Read each sentence one at a time and ask yourself after each one, is that correct? Then ask yourself, does it fit with the sentence before? Having got to the end of a paragraph ask yourself, do all the sentences in that paragraph belong there and do they relate to each other properly? Once you are happy with the sentences and paragraphs, run the spell checker and actively think about ways to remember each misspelling (see Chapter 8). Having done the spell check, read through again looking for words that are spelled correctly but are inappropriate grammatically. If you are not very good at proofreading then in the early stages you need to say to yourself, is that word correct? If the answer is yes, move on to the next word; if no, replace the word and start proofreading again at the beginning of the sentence. The same process has to be carried out to check punctuation as well. The good news is that if you work very slowly and methodically at first, then as you become better at proofreading you will get much quicker. A useful stage, if possible, is to ask someone who is better at proofreading than you, to have a look at it and for you to learn from their ideas by checking them against the information in books like this.

Proofreading test

OK, let's see how you do on a proofreading test. The following passage was written by a student. There are 11 errors – see if you can spot them all. The answers and explanation are below.

School-based Assignment for Maths

Assessment can take place over various periods of time, which can provide the teacher with different types of evidence. Short term assessment is an informal part of every day lessons. Used to check that children have understood the main teaching points of the session. Medium-term assessment is done every half term and relates to the programmes of study in the National Curriculum. Medium-term assessment is planned for and included in the end of term lessons. Long-term assessment is done at the end of the school year, to review and assess progress made by the children (National Numeracy Strategy, 1999).

There are two main forms of assessment used in school Firstly formative assessment which is an on going and informal assessment.

DOS AND DON'TS

✓ **Do**

- remember that effective presentation is often simple and logical
- understand the limitations of PowerPoint in addition to the advantages
- learn to type properly

✗ **Don't**

- leave the proofreading too close to the assignment deadline
- let worries about errors interrupt the flow of your writing in the early drafts
- forget the importance of legible handwriting for exams

Proofreading test answers

School-b[1]ased Assignment for Maths

Assessment can take place over various periods of time[2], which can provide the teacher with different types of evidence. Short term[3] assessment is an informal part of

(Continued)

(Continued)

every[4] day lessons.[5] Used to check that children have understood the main teaching points of the session. Medium-term assessment is done every half term and relates to the [6]programmes of study in the [7] National Curriculum. Medium-term assessment is planned for and included in the[8] end of term lessons. Long-term assessment is done at the end of the school year,[9] to review and assess progress made by the children (National Numeracy Strategy[10], 1999)[11]

[12]There are two main forms of assessment used in school Firstly[13] formative assessment which is an on[14] going and informal assessment.

1   'Based' in 'School-*Based*' should have a capital letter because it is in the title.
2   The comma in the first line is unnecessary. Although this is a structural point I don't think that this sentence is a good one for the start of the paragraph (or the start of an assignment). A better topic sentence for the paragraph might be 'Short-term, medium-term and long-term assessments provide the teacher with different types of evidence'. This is much more to the point and properly introduces the reader to what is to follow.
3   It should be 'Short-term' so it isn't confused with 'term assessment'.
4   It should be 'everyday'.
5   No full stop, capital letter, or other punctuation required here.
6   and 7 These are correct. National curriculum can be lower or upper case.
8   Probably better to delete 'the' but this is more a stylistic point than something which is a clear error.
9   The comma is not necessary.
10 This citation should be to the Department for Education and Skills, not to the title of the document.
11 A full stop is missing.
12 Leaving a line space between paragraphs is fine but first line indents with no space are more conventional in academic writing.
13 A capital letter at the beginning of 'Firstly' is incorrect. This might be a good point for a colon followed by the point about formative assessment and then a point about summative assessment. This could be done using 'firstly' and 'secondly' although I find this a bit old-fashioned. Another option is to use list features like '(a)' and '(b)', but the sentence would work fine with: 'There are two main forms of assessment used in school: formative assessment which is an ongoing informal type of assessment, and summative assessment which …'.
14 Should be 'ongoing'.

And that was only one paragraph plus a bit more. Don't worry if you are slow at first – as I have said, you will get quicker. If you really do not have time to proofread every word of an assignment to this level then make sure you look at the first page in particular. When examiners look at an assignment they often scrutinise the first page particularly carefully. If they find a lot of errors then they are more likely to look at the proofreading of the other pages.

10

Assessment and Learning from Feedback

Before you start work on an assignment, you must clearly understand what is expected and the criteria that will be used to mark the work. This chapter explains how assessment systems work by giving an example of a typical assignment. You are also shown two different kinds of feedback and given advice on how to learn from feedback.

Most universities now have quite a wide range of types of assessment. These include presentations, creative products with accompanying rationale, performances, and some courses even include online assessment forums. However, the most common form of assessment is a written assignment, or, in more traditional universities like Cambridge and Oxford, formal written examinations are the norm. But what nearly all these assessments have in common is the need for students to excel in writing. Even an oral presentation requires tight control of the structure of the presentation, meticulous planning that usually involves note-taking and recording, and attention to the meaning and elegance of the textual parts of the presentation. Although most of the examples in this book relate to written assessments, the skills that you will acquire in relation to academic writing are often applicable to other assessments that require any use of printed text. The ability to control written language is paramount in academic study and progression, as I hope this book has illustrated.

One of the most common causes of poor marks is the failure to understand the requirements of an assessment. Before you start work make sure that you clearly understand what is expected by reading and re-reading the information provided in the course handbooks. Pay close attention in any session where you are given guidance on assessment. If having done this and read the information carefully you are still unsure then make an appointment to see a tutor. A marker cannot give you any marks at all if you have not carried out what is required.

Assuming that you are clear about what is expected overall, you need to turn your attention to the assessment criteria; it is these that the marker will use to arrive at a judgement. Although all assignments will have assessment criteria, the way that these are represented, the number of criteria, and how the marker arrives at a judgement vary on different courses. One general idea that is common to all courses is the notion of progression. For example, for a degree course there is an expectation that the assessment demands for each year of study are progressively harder. Year one is often called level one, year two level two and year three level three.

There have been, and there continue to be, discussions about the distinctions between these levels (and other levels as you progress to postgraduate study). Rather than get bogged down in the detail of this now, here are some broad differences. Level-one degree work requires you to show a clear understanding of the main concepts related to the assessment topic and communicate this effectively through your writing. Level-two work requires you to demonstrate critical analysis in addition to showing clear understanding of the main concepts. At level three, the particular requirement, which builds on levels one and two, is that you can critically synthesise theory and evidence (for more discussion about how to demonstrate critical thinking see 'Critical reading and systematic recording' in Chapter 2, and 'critical thinking' later in this chapter).

 KEY FACT

Degree work

    Level one: Clear understanding of concepts
    Level two: Critical analysis
    Level three: Critical synthesis of theory and evidence

On some education courses, the assessment is either a pass or a fail. On other courses, a mark is awarded. Traditionally, degree course marking has used the following scale:

0 to 39 marks is equivalent to resubmission or a fail.
40 to 49 marks is equivalent to a third-class (III) degree.
50 to 59 marks is equivalent to a lower-second-class (II ii) degree (the most common).
60 to 69 marks is equivalent to an upper-second-class (II i) degree.
70 to 100 marks is equivalent to a first-class (I) degree.

There are general criteria for levels one, two and three which represent performance at these different classifications, but it is very hard to link these general criteria with work that you are doing for a particular assignment. This is why I recommend that you pay particularly careful attention to the advice given and the criteria established by your tutors for specific assignments.

Traditionally, markers for degree courses rarely give marks above 80. It is not entirely clear why this is, although to a certain extent it reflects the fact that all assignments could be improved in one way or another. It perhaps also reflects the fact that you cannot put all your effort into one assignment because you tend to be working on more than one task at any one time. This means that there is a compromise in the amount of time you can spend perfecting just one of the assignments.

The way that marks are awarded varies. Some courses clearly link performance with specific marks related to particular criteria. For example, if we had 10 assessment criteria for an assignment, it would be convenient to award a maximum of 10 marks per criterion. If it was decided to do that, you could have a scale like this:

outstanding – 9 or 10 marks
excellent – 7 or 8 marks
good – 5 or 6 marks
weak – 3 or 4 marks
very weak – 1 or 2 marks

A problem with detailed numeric marking systems like the one above is that some markers say these are too mechanistic and do not represent a realistic picture. For example, how could we justify that one student received six marks for a particular criterion whereas another student only received five marks? On the other hand, these kinds of systems clearly show the areas that are strong in an assignment and the areas that are weak. Some markers prefer broader indications such as strong, satisfactory and weak for each criterion, which can be indicated with a tick, rather than a number, which gets round the problem of being unrealistically specific.

An important thing to understand is that no matter how rigorous the marking process and its *moderation* ❺ are, a *subjective* judgement is made by a marker/examiner. This means that it is possible that you may occasionally receive a few marks more than you should have and sometimes you may receive a few marks less than you should have. Students are unlikely to be disadvantaged by this overall because final grades reflect averages of marks awarded across many assignments marked by many markers. All institutions also have ways to deal with borderline final classifications which can involve quite complicated calculations based on a range of assessment marks from different stages of the course. The subjective nature of the marking process is the reason why students cannot appeal against an examiner's judgement. They can appeal against an assessment only if examiners have not followed the correct procedures laid down by the course and the institution. If students could appeal against examiners' judgements, the whole system could become mired in endless arguments about marks and judgements. Markers already have to justify a proportion of their judgements through moderation with colleagues and external examiners.

KEY FACT

Moderation is the process of checking that assessments made by markers are accurate and fair.

KEY FACT

On average, 10 per cent of assignments are moderated in order to ensure standards of marking. Dissertation marking often has 100 per cent moderation because it contributes so much to the final degree classification.

Student example: rationale for a planned sequence of lessons

Let's look at an example of level-one work from a student who was in year one of a BA Education with Qualified Teacher Status degree. The assignment was as follows:

Plan a sequence of three lessons in your specialist subject area for the age-group that you are going to teach on your next school experience. Write three lesson plans in the recommended format and a 1000 word rationale for your lessons. In the rationale you should explain why the activities are suitable for the age-group that you have chosen. You should also explain the extent to which you think the activities will motivate the children you are going to teach. You should discuss the ways in which your planning is related to the national curriculum and/or national strategy.

The assessment criteria were as follows.
Specific criteria:

1 appropriateness of the activities
2 clarity of the links between learning objectives and the activities
3 imaginative planning of activities and resources
4 understanding of cross-curricular links
5 likelihood that activities will motivate children
6 understanding of links with the national curriculum and/or national strategy
7 evidence of reading to support rationale.

General level-one criteria:

8 clear understanding of concepts
9 well-structured submission (for example, sequence of ideas, paragraphs, headings)
10 effective presentation, proofreading, grammar and referencing.

This kind of assignment is common on education courses because it links work done on the course with school experience. One of its positive features is that it encourages preparation for and thought about teaching prior to work done with children. The disadvantage of this kind of assignment is that it is difficult to plan activities for children until you are working with them. Day-to-day assessments and evaluations make it much easier to plan because you have more informed knowledge about what the children will require next.

In view of what I said above about understanding what is required, if you only submitted two lesson plans for this assignment you would lose marks. If you did not submit the rationale you would probably only be able to achieve a maximum of about 25 marks out of 100, which would not be enough to pass. If you failed to show that you had done any background reading, you would score zero marks for criterion point seven and would lose marks for points six and ten.

Here are my suggestions for how you would meet the criteria. The choice of activities for the children is central to the assignment, hence criterion point one. If you are confident then you might use the knowledge that you already have to design your own activities. Those who are less confident would want to search the internet for ideas including government sites that support the different subjects (no matter how confident you are, this is a useful strategy to check what other teachers and academics are suggesting). There is a wealth of material here as well as many activity suggestions.

★ **TOP TIP**

Try the standards site at http://www.standards.dfes.gov.uk for teaching ideas supported by government.

Your activities would also need to show a logical sequence. Assessment criterion points three and five would be met if you showed that you had thought about ways that the activities would motivate children – this probably requires at least one paragraph per lesson in the rationale. Activity suggestions online can often be improved, in particular by thinking about what is more likely to motivate children in the context of the school you will be teaching in. This may also show your ability to think critically. Your lesson plan would need to show that links with other subjects had been made (point four). Points six and seven could be covered together through some background reading about the subject, including its place within the national curriculum and some of the key issues revealed in relevant publications.

A student who met the criteria very well on the task above received the following comments in their feedback sheet:

> The activities and resources that you have planned are imaginative and very likely to motivate the Year 2 children that you will be teaching. I particularly liked the puppet-show idea. Your comments about the benefits of drama were supported well by your background reading. You could have used some more sources to help you critically analyse some of the views that you put forward. Overall this was an excellent assignment.

Now let's look at a student who performed less well:

> You chose three activities that Year 4 children are likely to enjoy. Your comment about the range of approaches to mathematical addition was supported by a useful citation.

> Overall, there was a lack of evidence in the assignment that you had clearly understood the way that your activities fitted with the national curriculum. This may have been the reason that they lacked an appropriate sense of progression. You need to do more reading in order to ensure that you have a proper understanding of the topic. Please look again at the referencing guidelines and ensure that you follow these. There were a large number of proofreading errors.

One of the best ways to improve your writing and marks for assignments is to learn from feedback. The first thing to do is to carefully read the comments. This might sound obvious but some students do not do this because they just consider the overall mark. When you first read some critical comments, it is quite natural to go through these feelings:

- *irritation* – how dare they treat my work in this way!
- *denial* – surely there must be some mistake?
- *resigned acceptance* – I suppose I'd better read the comments.
- *new learning* – I have thought about each of the comments and some will help me improve in future.

You need to read each comment and look back at the assignment to decide whether you could have improved it. Then, most importantly, you need to think about how what you have learned from the feedback could help your next assignment. If you really do not understand why the comments have been made, you should make an appointment to see your tutor. Do not attend this meeting expecting to argue about the mark. It is far better if you take a notebook and jot down as many of the suggestions that the tutor gives you as you can, with a view to improving the resubmission if there is one and/or your next assignment.

Critical thinking

One of the most important aspects of academic study is the ability to apply critical thinking. Critical thinking means that you can weigh up *evidence* in a balanced way and then put forward a clear point of view. The word 'critical' in this context means not accepting things at face value. Critical thinking also reflects your ability to challenge your own ideas by evaluating them in relation to other people's work. Critical thinking may at times be based on reflections about your professional practice and/or reading of expert accounts of professional practice.

Critical thinking does not mean 'critical' in a negative sense, although negative critical comments are sometimes a necessary part of critical thinking. Critical thinking should become a characteristic of the way that you approach study in general, and is something that has to be demonstrated in your writing (which comes from thorough preparation, see Chapter 2). Critical thinking is the ability to reflect on ideas and to question them. It involves reflecting on theory, research and practice (revealed by authors in their publications), and offering alternative viewpoints. Critical thinking is often subtly revealed in students' writing, so it is quite difficult to give general advice on how to demonstrate it. However, having read the examples that follow, of an undergraduate degree essay and a master's degree essay, and the commentaries, I hope you will be in a better position to develop critical thinking yourself.

Student example: critical thinking in an essay on the aims of education

A group of third-year BA Education students were required to write an essay on the following: Critically discuss what you think should be the main aim of education. The essays were part of an educational philosophy module. They were formatively assessed by a supervisor who also led a small group discussion about the general features that the essays raised.

Stephanie's opening paragraph was as follows:

> Throughout history, many philosophers have debated the main aims of education, and many different theories have been expressed. Whilst philosophers such as Pring argue the fact that education should prepare children for the world of work, Dewey believes that education should enable social advancement, and encourages 'education for all'. **Ultimately however, these theories often reflect the time and place the philosophers were writing in, and thus some aims of education that have been theorised may not be relevant today.** To discuss the main aim of education, one must examine these theories, and apply them to modern times. However, **the question must also be asked whether there can only be one overarching aim to education, or whether there are many different kinds of educational aims.** If the latter is the case, then it must be discussed whether or not these aims are conflicting, or mutually consistent and self-supporting. [bold font added to show language that demonstrates criticality]

This is a confidently written first paragraph. The student had attended the relevant lectures, followed up the recommended reading, and hence showed a good level of knowledge that is necessary for critical thinking. The bold font examples represent the language that shows her initial critical thinking. However, to determine the quality of this thinking, ultimately it was necessary to follow her line of argument later in the essay as a whole to see if the promises of this first paragraph were achieved.

The idea of the time and place of philosophical writing was pursued very well in the main body of the essay. Stephanie briefly addressed the ideas of key philosophers of education from a range of periods, and showed her ability to think critically about their ideas. For example, the idea of the role of education to develop the rational mind was contrasted with the aim to enable people to be free, i.e. a democratic aim. This section in the essay was concluded with the following sentence: "and therefore could it be argued that the main aim of education is freedom, and that a sub aim of that is the production of rational thought, to give people the opportunity to be free?". This showed critical thinking and critical synthesis of large areas of intellectual thought – strong writing. A minor criticism was the use of the phrase "and therefore could it be argued": this is rather passive and perhaps reveals uncertainty in the line of argument, or it could simply be a mannerism of her writing. Although it is sometimes appropriate to be tentative, for example as part of the conclusions to a small-scale research study, in general a confident active tone of writing should be adopted. This is because most assessors understand that the argument is the opinion of the writer and do not expect this to be explicitly referred to. Stephanie might have been better to say, 'and therefore one of the main aims of education is ...'.

The supervisor regarded the essay overall as demonstrating work at the upper-second-class degree level. One of the feedback comments suggested how the student might improve to first-class degree level:

> You conclude that happiness should be the main aim of education but I'm not sure you provided sufficient argument and evidence in your essay for this conclusion. For example, you didn't write about the possible counter-arguments to your suggestion that development of the rational mind, coupled with allowance for natural development, and the development of 'skills education' will lead to happiness. One aspect you should have considered is that skills education when done inappropriately can make people unhappy.

One of the issues that was discussed with the whole group was the extent to which it is appropriate to regard the ideas of the philosopher John Dewey as synonymous with *child-centred education*. This discussion included reflection on the way that the media sometimes sloppily equate Dewey's *pragmatism* (in the philosophical sense) with 'letting children do what they want'. The supervisor had prepared a series of quotes from John Dewey's original work that clearly showed that this kind of media impression was false.

> Critical thinking is not a single attribute, it requires understanding of a range of aspects, not least the need for a convincing line of argument in any academic writing.

Assessment at master's degree level

Master's degrees are academically the next step after the first degree. Many postgraduate teacher-training courses offer the opportunity to gain qualifications at master's level as part of the course. This means that the assignments require a higher level of work, and hence different assessment criteria from those covered so far in the chapter will apply. The following is an example of criteria that are used to assess whether assignments and essays are at master's level. The criteria address six areas: (1) focus of the study; (2) knowledge and understanding; (3) development of an argument; (4) critical engagement and judgement; (5) structure and organisation; and (6) presentation. Areas five and six are covered in other chapters in this book so I will deal with areas one to four in this chapter.

1 Focus of the study

The most important aspect of making sure that your work meets this criterion is to ensure that the focus of the work is appropriately related to the assessment task. For some assessments, this criterion also requires you to show that you have read sufficiently about your field so were able to select an appropriate topic for research.

As I showed earlier, the easiest way to lose marks is to fail to follow the assessment requirements. Having selected an appropriate focus, it is important that this focus be clearly maintained throughout your writing. This is not as straightforward as it sounds because in the course of a sustained piece of writing at this level you are likely to deal with some philosophical and theoretical ideas when writing about an educational topic. Without care, philosophies and theories can become too prominent or lead the writing in different directions from the central focus. This is related to criteria point five on structure and organisation. An assignment or essay that is well structured will maintain at least one overall focus throughout, which anchors the writing for the reader and the writer.

2 Knowledge and understanding

This is really the main reason that assessments are set, to make sure that your knowledge and understanding are at the necessary level. The starting point for this is your understanding of the texts that you read which will support your writing. If you are not really clear about the meaning of an article or a section in a book, this will show in the way that you write about it. The notes that you keep after reading various texts are important and will need revisiting several times so that you are sure that you are representing other people's views accurately and with understanding (see Chapter 2). Defining terms is a starting point for knowledge and understanding. You have choices to make here because authors frequently define things in subtly different ways according to their views about the field of study.

A high level of understanding is shown through a strong grasp of the field of study. This includes understanding the central concepts and the debates. It can require both academic and professional/practical knowledge. For some assignments, you will need to show knowledge not only about the topic itself (something called the substantive area) but also about research methodology.

3 Development of an argument

This is one of the most challenging aspects of writing a good assignment. I have already said that one part of this is having a coherent focus throughout. But the most important feature of a well-argued piece is the way that evidence is used. Many people say that a good argument is one where the evidence is weighed up fairly on both sides. This is certainly true. However, although evidence from different perspectives must be evaluated it is important that you put forward a clear point of view after having addressed various sources of evidence. After you have read Chapter 1 on different sources of evidence such as articles, books and the internet, your argument will be stronger because you will be able to carefully select, and comment appropriately, on different types of evidence. Most educational topics require an argument that recognises complexities. Judgements that you make must be based on evidence, not assertions based on personal experience alone. In order to write a good argument, you also need to be very careful not to over-generalise. A good argument will arrive at clear conclusions that are related to the questions and/or issues that the writing seeks to address.

4 Critical engagement and judgement

This criterion is the hallmark of master's level work and beyond, and is one that I have addressed in this chapter and in Chapter 2. It is not enough to write descriptive accounts; you will need to show that you have engaged with sources of evidence and theory. The claims and arguments made by the authors that you read and cite need to be subjected to your critical judgement. This means that you have to clearly understand the points that other authors make, think about them in relation to your own view and the views of other writers, and then present your points in the light of this thinking. You also need to think about the reasons you selected particular sources and not others, and the reasons you cover some topics and not others. Your reflections on practice, research and theory should be analytical and not merely descriptive. You need to try and anticipate possible lines of objection to your argument and show how this affects your position. You also need to show awareness of the significance and implications of your argument. The strongest writing also shows some original characteristics in its arguments.

The separation of the criteria into categories helps you to see the different elements that are involved in good writing at master's level. However, as you may have seen in the descriptions of the categories, the boundaries between them are not as clear-cut as a numbered list suggests. Frequently, in order to clearly meet one criterion, you have to take account of another. When you begin drafting your assignments, you will need the support of a supervisor to help you understand how your writing can address the criteria.

Student example: master's level criteria addressed in an essay showing reflections on a published research paper

One of the essays for a master's degree required students to select a research paper to analyse in order to review some of the major approaches to educational research and the underlying philosophical issues. First, I show a short example from a draft of Ingrid's writing and then some feedback that was offered.

> In this short essay I aim to explore the major approaches to educational research through looking at a paper by Julie Martello, an Australian early years researcher. I place it within the interpretivist paradigm and through subsequent discussion use it to highlight some of the issues and debate amongst the different traditions. First, however, in order to provide some sort of beginning context for this essay, I offer a brief synopsis of what a paradigm is in relation to research in general and educational research in particular; 'research is concerned with understanding the world and … this is informed by how we view our world(s), what we take understanding to be, and what we see as the purposes of understanding'. (Cohen, Manion and Morrison, 2004, p. 3)
>
> As suggested by the above quote, each paradigm comes with its own distinct epistemology or conceptualisation (philosophy) of the world. Each has its own consensus or approved ways of collecting empirical data that can be analysed usefully and constructively with a view to furthering our knowledge and understanding of the social reality in which we live. Whilst every paradigm seeks to discover or uncover Truth, how that truth is verified or validated is the subject of much heated debate amongst the protagonists of each position.

The following feedback was discussed at a tutorial. It was presented as a single block of text but, for the purposes of this chapter, I have divided it into the numbered criteria in order to illustrate them.

1 Focus of the study

> "Give the reader a bit more information about the findings/conclusions of the paper that you are using as a stimulus for the assignment."

If an assignment requires you to comment in depth about a research paper like this, it is important that you give the reader enough information about the original paper for them to evaluate your reflections.

2 Knowledge and understanding

"Be absolutely clear about what the different philosophical terms mean. Decide which ones you want to use and don't hedge your bets with unnecessary alternatives, e.g. 'epistemology or conceptualisation (philosophy)' – each of these three words [epistemology/conceptualisation/ philosophy] has a distinct meaning."

When you are faced with many new terms to understand, it can be common to use more than one term, partly as a misguided way of trying to show knowledge. This strategy often reflects a lack of confidence and a related lack of understanding of the different terms. Terms should be seen as convenient ways to represent different complex ideas, and for this reason you need to decide which terms you are going to use in preference to others, and stick to them throughout your writing.

3 Development of an argument

"Deal with the main paradigm debate once, don't keep repeating this kind of information. Try and avoid secondary references. Locate original sources in the library and read them. Don't overuse one source such as Pring. Follow up his references."

The debates about different kinds of research, such as qualitative and quantitative, frequently feature in thinking about educational research. But it is important that these kinds of issues are given appropriate weight in an essay and not repeated unnecessarily (unless the debate is the central focus of your work).

4 Critical engagement and judgement

"I don't think that covering three other paradigms towards the end of the paper is a good idea. You deal with them all too superficially – particularly critical theory. I'm tempted to say you should decide on one to cover in more depth. For example action research could include Lewin's (1946) seminal definition for which I have his paper. John Elliot's work has also been influential. If you want to try and make the difficult link between practice and postmodernism I would recommend looking at Stronach and MacClure's book."

Writing superficially about complex ideas is another thing that you should constantly be on your guard against. The difficulty is often to do with choices about what to omit rather than what to include. In order to give enough space to write about a complex idea you need to decide not to cover other ideas – this requires you to make judgements based on your reading of different sources.

5 Structure and organisation

"I'm not sure that explaining the aim of the essay is a good first paragraph. What about something like the start of para 3? In the second or third para you could explain aim of essay – but do this only once."

6 Presentation

Presentation issues were not discussed at this tutorial.

Feedback happens to us all

Just in case you are thinking that it is only students who have to deal with feedback, here is an example which shows that tutors have to as well. When I submit a paper to a journal, it goes out to anonymous referees who are experts in the field. The better journals send you copies of these referees' reports along with the editor's decision about the paper (frequently this process takes months). I once sent a paper called 'The National Literacy Strategy: a critical review of empirical evidence' to an American journal called *Reading Research Quarterly*. It was sent out to four referees but the decision overall was split between those who wanted to accept and those who wanted more work on the paper or who thought it should be rejected. The editors suggested some changes be made and that it then be sent to a second group of referees, although the most critical referee from the first round was also used for the second round. By the end of the second round of reports, there was still opinion both for and against publication. On the positive side were comments like this:

The argument produced in this paper is an exemplary contribution in the manner of the educational researcher as public intellectual. A lot of high-sounding stuff has been written about 'public intellectuals', but this paper instantiates a highly plausible and responsible act of public intellectualism. The author has demonstrated that policy interventions and implementations can be challenged on their own terms, by means of careful scholarship and critical engagement with empirical evidence. This is a heartening paper, and it should prove also to be an encouraging paper for people working at the chalk face in literacy education throughout the English-speaking world. We have all endured the kinds of 'reforms' exemplified by the NLS and its FFT. There are many teachers trying to work to the limits of their capacity and integrity under conditions they experience as inappropriate and not in the best interests of many learners. These people look to educational researchers to provide forms of critique and leadership that hold out hope for more expansive and balanced policy directions.

This paper gives such teachers something to look to. It provides a role model for other literacy researchers. And it is the kind of careful, measured, fair-minded and well-conceived research-based article we can never have too much of. (Anonymous referee, 2002)

My grateful thanks to that reviewer! But now look at the following comment about the very same paper:

1   I am not convinced that the attack on Beard is tackled in a fundamentally new manner; the argument is sound, but it has been heard for over two years from Hilton in the UK.

2   Stripped of its sweeping claims regarding alternative strategies, the paper is leaner, but relatively brief, and contains little that would be new for a UK audience. The points about the teaching of grammar are sound, but Beard himself quotes much of this evidence – it's just that he then goes on to spend 50 pages in his book telling how to deliver the teaching of grammar.

3   The author's final point is a call for an 'urgently needed' new review that critically examines research and practice, and how the two are linked. The government did indeed commission such a review in 2001, and it was published in June this year (see Harrison, 2002). (Anonymous referee, 2002)

In the end, the editors' decision was to reject the paper (for more information about the story of this paper, see Wyse, 2004). However, this was not the end of the story. I submitted the paper to *The British Educational Research Journal* (*BERJ*). Once again the referees disagreed. One suggested urgent publication with only minor changes, the other suggested rejection. On this occasion, the editors, having read the paper themselves, felt that the positive reviewer's view should prevail so they recommended publication on the proviso that the negative reviewer could offer an article in the same edition of the journal, challenging the views that I put forward. It turned out that the negative reviewer was the person who wrote the government publication that I was critical about in my paper.

I went through all the stages from irritation to new learning that I outlined above (several times), just as you may when you receive comments about your assignments. I learned least from the most critical reviewer for *Reading Research Quarterly*, and after some thought rejected their comments because I felt they were affected more by their personal perspective than an objective consideration of the issues. I learned a great deal from the reviewers who appeared genuinely open-minded and rigorous. Although accepting critical feedback is difficult, it can also be exhilarating once you clearly see that some of the points really are important and will help you to learn more.

To conclude this chapter, and the book, I want to leave you with a particularly happy ending! One of the students who I worked with carried out a piece of small-scale research, which she wrote up as an assignment. She had been working with a child in a reception class who was described as a 'selective mute' – a child who decides not to speak. Such children are challenging for teachers because so much learning happens through spoken interaction. Even the experienced teacher who the student was working with had struggled to support the child. The student took the opportunity to relate the practical situation to her final research assignment. She searched for research about the condition and was able to use this to develop strategies that she hoped would benefit the child. By the end of her teaching practice, the child had started some limited talk with the student. This was a tremendous achievement. My comments about the assignment were enthusiastic, partly because she had addressed the criteria very well but also because it was one of the best assignments I had ever read:

> This really was an outstanding piece of work. The integration of theory and practice was a delight. It was helped by the fact that this was a real problem that you wanted to solve but I think this assignment demonstrates that research, theory and practice in combination offer a powerful tool for addressing problems in the classroom. It has also taught me much and I would like to keep this as an example for future students. Well done!

I hope that your own hard work and talent, coupled with some of the ideas learned from this book, will help you to achieve similarly positive feedback!

DOS AND DON'TS

✓ **Do**

- make sure you clearly understand the assessment requirements
- learn from any sessions which are designed to support your planning for the assignment
- read feedback and learn from it

(Continued)

(Continued)

✗ Don't

- forget to check that you are addressing all the assessment criteria
- look at the mark for an assignment and not the feedback
- assume that you cannot improve in future if you have struggled with an assignment

Further Reading

Andrews, R. (2009). *Argumentation in Higher Education: Improving Professional Practice through Theory and Research*. London: Routledge.
Richard Andrews has devoted much of his academic work to the study of written argument so his thoughts are well worth considering.

Creme, P., & Lea, M. (2003). *Writing at University: A Guide for Students*. Maidenhead: Open University Press.
A classic text for the support of students.

Gourevitch, P. (Ed.). (2007). *The Paris Review Interviews* [three volumes]. Edinburgh: Canongate.
Wonderful accounts by writers of their craft.

Kamler, B., & Thomson, P. (2006). *Helping Doctoral Students to Write: Pedagogies for Supervision*. London: Routledge.
Particularly good on the social and cultural aspects of academic writing at doctoral level.

King, S. (2000). *On Writing: A Memoir of the Craft*. London: Hodder and Stoughton.
Stephen King, of some famous horror books, is very good on the craft of writing.

Lavelle, E., & Zuercher, N. (2001). The writing approaches of university students. *Higher Education*, 42, 373–391.
One example of the research that is being carried out into university students' writing.

Lea, M., & Street, B. (2006). The 'academic literacies' model: Theory and applications. *Theory into Practice*, 45(4), 368–377.
A theory of academic writing.

Smith, F. (1994). *Writing and the Writer* (2nd edition). Hillsdale, NJ: Lawrence Erlbaum.
A provocative but thoughtful book about the processes of writing that writers go through.

References

Alderson, P. (1995). *Listening to Children: Children, Ethics and Social Research*. Ilford: Barnardos.

Alderson, P. and Morrow (2011). *The Ethics of Research with Children and Young People: A Practical Handbook*. London: SAGE.

American Psychological Association. (2009). *Publication Manual of the American Psychological Association* (6th edition). Washington, DC: American Psychological Association.

Barber, C. (1993). *The English Language: A Historical Introduction*. Cambridge: Cambridge University Press.

Bryson, B. (1990). *Mother Tongue: The English Language*. London: Penguin Books.

Buzan, T. (2003). *The Speed Reading Book*. London: BBC Books.

Carter, J. (1999). *Talking Books: Children's Authors Talk about the Craft, Creativity and Process of Writing*. London: Routledge.

Crystal, D. (1997). *The Cambridge Encyclopedia of Language* (2nd edition). Cambridge: Cambridge University Press.

Crystal, D. (2004). *The Stories of English*. London: Penguin/Allen Lane.

Department for Education and Skills (DfES) (2003) *Excellence and Enjoyment: A Strategy for Primary Schools*. Suffolk: DfES.

Greenbaum, S. (1986). Spelling variants in British English. *Journal of English Linguistics*, 19, 258–268.

Higher Education Funding Council for England, Scottish Higher Education Funding Council, Higher Education Funding Council for Wales, and Department for Employment and Learning Northern Ireland (2005). *Rae 2008 Research Assessment Exercise: Guidance to Panels*. Retrieved July 2005, from http://www.rae.ac.uk/pubs/ 2005/01/ rae0105.doc

Kirby, P. (1999). *Involving Young Researchers: How to Enable Young People to Design and Conduct Research*. York: York Publishing Services.

Peters, M. (1985). *Spelling Caught or Taught: A New Look* (revised edition). London: Routledge.

Pyles, T., & Algeo, J. (1993). *The Origins and Development of the English Language* (4th edition). London: Harcourt Brace Jovanovich.

Sassoon, R. (2003). *Handwriting: The Way to Teach It* (2nd edition). London: Paul Chapman Publishing.

Smith, F. (1994). *Writing and the Writer* (2nd edition). Hillsdale, NJ: Lawrence Erlbaum.

Tufte, E. R. (2003). *The Cognitive Style of PowerPoint*. Cheshire, CT: Graphics Press LLC.

Tymms, P. (2004). Are standards rising in English primary schools? *British Educational Research Journal*, 30(4), 477–494.

University of Cambridge Board of Graduate Studies. (2007, 3 August 2006). *Plagiarism*. Retrieved 22 April 2007, from http://www.admin.cam.ac.uk/offices/gradstud/current/submitting/plagiarism.html

Wyse, D. (2004). And they all lived happily ever after? The story of a paper. *Research Intelligence*, 86, 4–8.

Glossary

The definitions below refer to their use within the context of this book.

American Psychological Association (APA) 6th Style A set of conventions for writing academic papers, including referencing, that have been set out in a book by the American Psychological Association.

Anecdotal evidence Information that we gather in our daily lives that informs our beliefs about the world.

Author/date system A way of referring to texts. The author's surname is followed by the year of publication.

Bibliography/annotated bibliography An alphabetic list at the end of a text which gives all the information that a reader needs if they want to read the texts that the author has referred to. It includes items that were read for but not cited in the text. An annotated bibliography is a bibliography with descriptive notes about the text after the entry in the list.

British Education Index A search tool dedicated to education that enables you to find educational papers more efficiently.

Citation A citation is part of a reference. It is included as part of a sentence in a text and is shown by an author's surname and the year of publication of their text. A citation may or may not include a direct quote.

Consent or assent form A form which is filled in by participants in research to show that they agree to take part and that they understand the consequences of taking part.

Coordinator A coordinator is a word which links parts of a sentence. The most common coordinators are 'and', 'or' and 'but'.

Critical analysis Analysis that involves weighing up evidence in a balanced way. Critical analysis reflects the ability to challenge ideas by evaluating them in relation to published work.

Dissertation An extended piece of formal writing which explores a topic in depth and is usually based upon original research. The term is related to the word 'discourse'.

Et al. Literally means 'and others'. Can be used to shorten a reference to a text with many authors.

Field An academic area of study.

Grammarian, descriptive People who see language as something to be described and analysed in order to understand the way that it is used. Descriptive grammarians are interested in the way that all language use reflects a particular context, such as the social background of the speaker and the setting in which the message is communicated.

Grammarian, prescriptive People who believe that there is a fixed set of grammatical rules which you have to learn in order to speak and write correctly.

Handbook A book which is typically international in scope and so has contributors from around the world who are experts in the field. It attempts to be comprehensive in order to establish a clear picture of the field at a particular moment in time.

Hyperlink A word or picture in an electronic document which is electronically linked to another document, or a place in the same document.

Ibid. In full, this is 'ibidem', which can be abbreviated to ibid. or ib. It literally means in the same place, often meaning in the same text as mentioned before. Like *op. cit.* this is used to avoid repeating a citation.

Inter-library loan A library service which allows you to borrow books or receive photocopies of journal articles that are not available in your university or college library.

Jargon Often used negatively to mean unusual words and phrases which confuse people. All areas of study use jargon to succinctly sum up ideas that will be understood by the expected audience.

Keyword A word which is used during searches to access documents that are related to the keyword or which contain the keyword.

Loanwords Words from other languages that have entered the English language.

Moderation The process of agreeing whether assessment procedures are accurate.

Op. cit. Located in the text (or other work) previously mentioned.

Paper An article published in an academic journal. Some papers are presented at academic conferences prior to publication.

Peer review A process designed to assess the quality of research papers. Papers are sent to experts in the field, who read them and then recommend publication or not.

Prefix A prefix consists of a letter or letters placed at the front of a word or stem to form a new word: for example, in 'before'/'be-fore', 'be' is the prefix and 'fore' is the stem.

Primary source The original text, one that has been read first hand.

Reference list An alphabetic list at the end of a text which gives all the information that a reader needs if they want to read the texts that the author has referred to.

Retrospective plan A retrospective plan is one that is written after you have done a draft of writing. It involves updating a plan after a draft.

Search A systematic way to find texts.

Search engine A piece of software which enables you to find particular information by using keywords. It is usually applied to internet searches.

Secondary source Referring to a text by using another author's reference to the text because you have not read the original first hand.

Sentence A language construction which can be used on its own, without people feeling that it is incomplete. It is the largest construction to which the rules of grammar apply. It is constructed according to a system of rules which are naturally acquired by nearly all the mother-tongue speakers of the language (Crystal, 2004, p. 37).

Sic Literally means 'thus'. It is used to refer to a word which looks unconventional or questionable but which is quoted exactly as it was in the original version of another text.

Speed-reading A technique which enables people to read much quicker than normal.

Spell checker A software function in a word processor which checks spellings.

Subheadings Headings which consist of words and phrases used to divide text into sections.

Suffix A suffix consists of a letter or letters placed at the end of a word or stem to form a new word: for example, in 'shorten'/'short-en', 'short' is the stem and 'en' is the suffix.

Theory Ideas which explain and summarise things. In research, theory is developed or confirmed by observation and experiment.

Track Changes A software function in a word processor which shows when changes have been made to a document.

Index

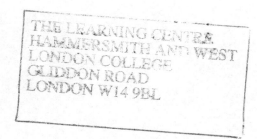